37 50

A guide to horse riding

A GUIDE TO HORSE RIDING

by

Lesley Eccles
'Horse & Pony Magazine'

Patrick Stephens

First published in 1988

British Library Cataloguing in Publication Data

Eccles, Lesley
    A guide to horse riding.
    1. Horsemanship
    I. Title
    798.2'3   SF309

    ISBN 1-85260-004-7

With grateful thanks to Mr and Mrs D. Ward,
the staff and students at Brampton Stables,
Church Brampton, Northampton, for their help
with the photographs.

*Patrick Stephens Limited is part of the
Thorsons Publishing Group, Wellingborough,
Northamptonshire, NN8 2RQ, England*

Printed in Great Britain by Woolnough
Bookbinding Limited, Irthlingborough,
Northamptonshire

10   9   8   7   6   5   4   3   2   1

CONTENTS

STARTING TO RIDE

Just imagine the pleasures of riding on long summer evenings; splashing through rivers and enjoying exhilarating gallops, exploring exciting new areas of the countryside, seeing deer, rabbits, pheasants and a host of other wildlife at close range — riding horses allows you all this and much more. By learning to ride you are setting off on an exciting journey, for the world of horses is challenging, varied and fascinating, and is open to anyone to enjoy.

Few people regret starting to ride. It can be a very sociable sport, with lots of new friends to be made, or it can be just you and the horse. The whole family can join in too, if you wish, taking part in picnic rides, holidays, visits to shows and so on. For some the rewards of riding are in thrilling pursuits such as cross-country riding or hunting, while others prefer the gentler pleasures of riding horses; the company of the animal and the peace of the countryside is enough.

Whichever you prefer, you can be sure that your new sport will stretch you physically and mentally. As it is such a physical activity regular riding will increase your fitness, but it will not only be your body which is exercised. Your mind will also do its share — working out how the horse ticks. Why is it that someone else always seems to get more out of a particular horse than you do? How does the horse always know if you are secretly worried about a certain jump?

Learning to understand horses and mastering the skills of riding will give you a tremendous sense of achievement, as once impossible movements become second nature. But there are always new skills to tax you, different horses to ride . . . the enjoyment and challenge of riding is endless.

In Britain, thousands upon thousands of people of all ages and from all social classes ride. At one time riding was very much a sport for the rich as only they could afford to keep horses. Now as well as valuable racehorses and eventers, there are thousands of ordinary animals, so riding is available to all.

In addition to the pleasure they give to able-bodied riders, horses also play a major part in enriching the lives of disabled people. The benefits to them are tremendous — for some it is the first time they have been able to move about without being in a wheel-chair. There are Riding for the Disabled Association (RDA) groups where adults and children can ride throughout Britain. With increasing leisure time and a growing awareness of the importance of exercise for continued good health, more and more people are turning to sport. It is not surprising that riding horses is a popular activity, because horses have always played a major part in man's history. Our ancestors rode to war on horseback, used them as pack animals, trained them to draw ploughs, carriages and to carry the mail. Yet horses have always been more than mere servants of man. Through the centuries writers, artists and poets have referred to the grace, strength, courage and beauty of the horse. These animals are part of our heritage and once again are becoming part of our daily lives.

The pleasure of knowing and riding horses is open to you — just take the first step and learn to ride.

Choosing a riding school

You can decide where to ride very easily. Just pick up the Yellow Pages, find the list of riding establishments, close your eyes and bring your pen to rest on one of the telephone numbers. Then just book a lesson and you're off!

It is just possible that you will find exactly what you want, but you could find yourself mounted on a scrawny animal too small for you and being yelled at by some youngster who mistakenly believes that she is teaching you. Unfortunately there are some doubtful 'riding schools' where the major object is to get as much as possible out of the animals as cheaply as possible, with no concern for them or the clients.

Your first riding experiences ought to give you a good springboard for an enjoyable future, so it is wise to select your school carefully. There is no reason either why you shouldn't change instructors or schools if your centre seems suitable at first but then fails to meet your needs.

Recommendation of a school is fine, providing you know other riders in the first place and as long as they are looking for the same from their hobby as you are. Everyone has different standards so do not feel pressurized into going along with your friend if she is happy riding at the local 'cowboy' outfit and you want to learn properly.

The first obstacle is knowing exactly what you want from your lessons. Are you learning to ride simply so you can enjoy riding out in the countryside, or do you hope to go on to greater things, like competitions and hunting? Are you fulfilling a lifetime's ambition in learning to ride, and does that ambition include the goal of having your own horse? Are you naturally a cautious, nervous person? Could you cope with being pushed into achieving more, or do you only respond to slow, encouraging tuition? Would it bother you if the animals you rode were not properly cared for, or would you boycott such a place and pay a couple of pounds more at a better school?

Of course your answers to the above may change with time. You may start riding simply to enjoy country life, but become so hooked that you eventually have your own horse.

Other factors are going to have a bearing on your choice of school. If you are a city dweller the number of riding places may be limited anyway so you will have to compromise. A local school may be ideal for the basics of riding but as you become more advanced you may have to travel further afield for tuition.

You will find details of schools local to you in the Yellow Pages, advertisements in your local newspaper and probably in any saddlers' shops in your vicinity. If you live in a tourist centre, try the Information Bureau too. Also available is *Where to Ride*, a booklet published annually by the British Horse Society (BHS), and the *Association of British Riding Schools (ABRS) Handbook.* These two publications list schools throughout Britain which are approved by the two organizations.

From all these sources you ought to have a selection of places to visit. Try to look at all the schools before booking a ride. Remember that as Saturday and Sunday are normal working days for a riding school they are often closed for one day during the week. Monday is a popular day off but check by telephone first if you want to visit a school in the week.

So what are you looking for when you walk into a riding school? First impressions, while not the be-all and end-all, are important. Does the place look reasonably neat and tidy? Are the staff friendly and helpful? Is there a cheerful working atmosphere or does the owner's miserable approach to life rub off on all and sundry?

As a potential customer you should be treated courteously. Say you are interested in having lessons and ask when a lesson could be arranged, how much lessons cost and how you will be taught.

There are different ways of teaching beginners, the best and safest way being to have a lunge lesson. You will have the instructor to yourself and will ride a horse which has been trained to move around the instructor in a large circle at the end of the lunge line. It is via this lunge line and her voice that the instructor controls the horse. The rider can therefore concentrate on getting the feel of riding a horse without worrying about where the horse is going.

Not all schools have the animals or staff to offer this ideal introduction to riding, so you will probably find yourself joining a class lesson. This will involve a small group of beginners and an instructor with helpers. While the instructor has overall control of the class each beginner

Lunge lessons give you a good start on the path to competent and confident riding. You will develop a feel for the way the horse moves and you will soon realize that you do not need the reins in order to balance.

should have a helper to lead the horse and generally assist them.

An old-fashioned way of teaching a beginner is by riding out on a lead rein. Both you and your instructor are mounted, with the instructor leading your horse.

Bear in mind that your first lessons are likely to last for just thirty minutes, as the concentrated physical activity makes your muscles tired.

Having established that the school can cater for you, ask whether you may borrow a hard hat from them. Some schools make a small charge for the use of hats, others supply them free for the first couple of lessons, but no school or instructor should allow you to ride without a hat.

If the school is not too busy when you visit ask if anyone is free to show you around. Some owners will arrange an escorted tour, while others will be happy to let you find your own way. Use this opportunity to inspect the horses, tack and facilities but do be careful when approaching horses (see later chapter for information on handling horses).

The tack room is where all the saddles, bridles and other equipment for the horses is kept. Everything should be neatly stored on racks with the horse's name alongside. Have a good look at the leather; it should be supple and well cared for, not hard and cracked, and the stitching

Saddlery should be good quality and well cared for. The tack room, where all the horsey equipment is stored, is often a hive of activity.

and buckles on all tack should be sound, too. Keeping everything clean in a busy centre is a continuous job so don't expect everything to be absolutely spotless all the time. However, tack which is always dirty and caked with mud is uncomfortable for the horse to wear and suggests that the school may fall down on other areas of care too.

Now to the horses and ponies. They may be kept in stables, stalls, crew yards or paddocks, but whichever method or combination of ways is employed, all the animals should be well covered with flesh, look healthy and be taking an interest in life. There are some animals who always tend towards leanness even though they are well fed, but if the whole equine population of the school looks scrawny then beware. Animals with their ribs showing, protruding haunches and overgrown feet are in poor condition and should not be expected to work until their health has improved.

You would expect stables (also known as loose boxes) to house just one horse or pony. Horses need stables about 4.3 × 3.7 metres (14 × 12 feet) while ponies need boxes about 3.7 × 3 metres (12 × 10 feet), although very small ponies can manage with a little less space. If the stables are significantly smaller than these dimensions, then the animals are going to be cramped.

Sometimes a building is divided into stalls. Each horse or pony has its own space but it is not free to move around at will. All the animals face a wall to which they are fastened by means of a headcollar and

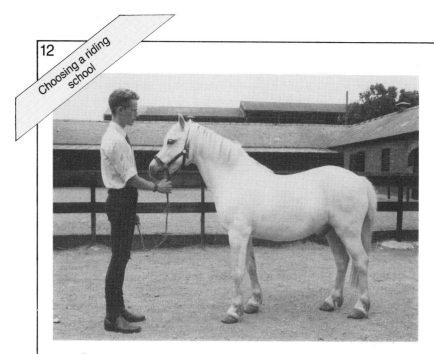

rope. Some schools provide divisions between each animal using walls or suspended wooden planks. Often stalls are used to house ponies who are out at grass overnight and brought into the yard during the day.

Crew yards are large enclosed areas usually with some covered shelter along one or more walls, in which several animals are kept together. The horses or ponies can move around at will.

Above A nice kind pony who is in good condition. Animals should be well-covered in flesh — if your local riding school keeps scrawny, thin ponies, then do not patronize the school.

Left Stables need to have ample bedding as shown here, with straw banked up the walls, to provide a comfortable and safe home for its occupant.

Right Feed stores need to be kept scrupulously clean, with feed bowls scrubbed after use and metal or other vermin-proof containers used to store the feed.

Paddocks, gates and fencing around the riding school should be in good order. Dangerous items, such as loose wire, should not be left lying around, and stable tools such as wheelbarrows, forks and brooms should be stored neatly out of the way so that neither animals nor young children are in danger of injuring themselves.

The accommodation for the animals should have ample bedding, either straw, shavings or paper. A thin layer across a stable floor is not enough. Bedding should be clean too — horses should not be left to stand for days on wet, soiled bedding. Some people do not provide bedding on the stable floor at all during the day so the animal has to stand for hours on concrete. This is not a very good practice as leaving horses like this does not encourage them to stale; many animals will hold on until they are on a softer surface. A lack of bedding also means that the horse is unable to lie down comfortably and rest when it wishes. Every day soiled and wet bedding should be transferred from the stables to the muck-heap, which needs to be kept under control; it should not resemble a sprawling disaster area!

All horses and ponies need clean water available at all times and hay should be given to the animals at intervals throughout the day in addition to their short feed of oats, sugar beet etc. Feed for the horses should be stored in a separate room, where cleanliness and tidiness are again the order of the day. Look out for the barn where the hay and straw are stored; suitable fire notices and extinguishers ought to be present.

If everything is fine so far, the next question is where will you ride?

An indoor arena is great as you can ride whatever the weather but as they are expensive not all schools will possess them. An enclosed outdoor riding area is therefore needed, because it is not safe to teach beginners in huge open spaces. Whether covered or outdoor, the arena should be about 40 × 20 metres (130 × 65 feet) to be a decent working size.

Hopefully you should be able to see a variety of coloured poles and jump wings for use in lessons. Depending on the school's land you may also see some fixed jumps dotted around the fields like a small cross-country course.

If possible, try to watch a lesson in progress to give you a chance to see the style of teaching in action and to acclimatize yourself before your first lesson.

You may notice signs around the school proclaiming that the school is approved or recognized by various organizations. These include the British Horse Society (BHS), Association of British Riding Schools (ABRS), Ponies of Britain (POB), Pony Trekking and Riding Society of Wales (PTRSW) and the Scottish Trekking and Riding Association (STRA). If a school is approved by one or more of these bodies it means that the establishment is checked regularly by representatives of the society to ensure that the standard of horse care and instruction is at a satisfactory level.

Not all schools are members of these societies but any riding school has to be licensed by the local authority so if conditions are particularly bad at any centre you visit, make sure your local council is aware of the problem.

The various equestrian societies are also involved in the training of instructors, grooms and pony trekking guides. The BHS qualifications are the ones you are most likely to come across. At the lowest level there is the British Horse Society Assistant Instructor (BHSAI) and this is the most common qualification. The next step is the Intermediate Instructor (BHSII), followed by the Instructor (BHSI), while a Fellow of the British Horse Society (FBHS) is the highest level. There are only a small number of Fellows in this country. For a newcomer to riding, instruction from a good BHSAI ought to be sufficient.

After you have visited a few schools, decide which is right for you. It may be the small school which offers highly individual personal attention or perhaps the larger school with the chance to ride more horses and take part in mini competitions. Just remember that riding is meant to be enjoyable so it is important that you feel welcome and wanted at your riding school.

Fitness

Once you've booked your introductory lesson, or even before, you can start to prepare for your first moments on horseback. To newcomers, and especially those who have not exercised recently, riding is quite a demanding sport, so it is worth easing your body gently into work before you even get on a horse.

As with any sport, the older you are when you start the more careful you must be not to push yourself too hard. Consult your doctor first if you are at all concerned about your health. Riding is a suitable hobby for all ages and all levels of fitness but new riders often find that they suffer from stiffness and aching leg and back muscles. Overweight riders also find that they easily become short of breath. So, what can you do to help your general fitness level before you start riding?

One of the best all round exercises, combining all the basic elements of suppleness, stamina and strength, is swimming. It is particularly beneficial because your weight is supported by the water and so there is less chance of straining a muscle.

Brisk walking is another good introduction to exercise, especially if it is some time since you did anything strenuous. Skipping and running up stairs are also useful. As with anything, start gently and build up gradually. Stop if you feel uncomfortable and never overdo it so that you feel distressed or are struggling to breathe properly.

When you start riding you will carry out exercises on horseback, but some of these can also be used on the ground to help improve your suppleness. Remember to loosen up your body first and allow your body to cool down gradually after your exercise session. Jogging on the spot, skipping or dancing away to a favourite record will help to warm up your muscles in preparation while a soak in the bath afterwards will help soothe any stiff muscles. A selection of exercises is listed below.

Exercises

Start at the top with head rolls. Let your head tilt forward so that your chin is resting on your chest and then slowly roll your head round and back, reaching over your shoulders without causing any discomfort and returning to the original position. Carry out this exercise in both clockwise and anticlockwise directions.

Now move on to the shoulders. Bring up both shoulders as if you are trying to touch your ears. Roll your shoulders back and downwards. Breathe in as you lift your shoulders and out as you execute the second half of the exercise.

To work your shoulder, wrist and elbow joints at the same time, sit on a chair with your arms held out to the side. Sit with your elbows 'inside out' so that the palms of your hands face the ceiling. Now turn your arms the right way round again. Repeat this exercise several times.

Arm circling next. Stand up, feet comfortably apart (about your shoulders' width), then lift up one arm in front of you, bringing it slowly up, backwards and around to describe a full circle. Repeat the exercise with the other arm and then try both together. You'll feel your body stretch as you circle your arms.

Now put your hands on your hips, and still standing with feet about shoulders' width apart, swivel your upper body round to the right, then to the left. Keep the lower half of your body as still as possible.

Let your arms hang relaxed by your sides and without tipping your body forward reach down your left leg as far as possible with your left hand. Then swap sides and reach down your right leg with your right hand. Inch your body down in either direction, without forcing yourself too much. After a short while you'll be able to reach further.

Time to touch your toes, but with a slight variation. Stand up, feet comfortably apart, and then reach down to touch your right foot with your left hand, left foot with your right hand. Return to an upright position each time before touching the other foot. You will probably not be able to reach your foot at first — just stretch down as far as you can. As you become more supple you'll find the exercise easier. Bending your knees is cheating!

Beginners often find it difficult to swing their legs high enough for mounting a horse so try this: using a chair back for support, swing one leg backwards and forwards, letting your leg go as far in each direction as possible. Try to keep your body vertical.

Finally — and this is much the easiest of the exercises — rotate your ankles while you are sitting in a chair.

Start off by practising these exercises fairly slowly, with five repetitions to begin with. For more fitness information and exercises, consult one of the many books or magazines now available.

What to wear

For your first lessons no-one will expect a beginner to have all the correct riding wear, so just dress sensibly. Loose fitting trousers are better than tight jeans, and a jumper or jacket which does not restrict your movement is ideal. It's vital to wear a British Standards Institute Approved riding hat and to fasten the chin-strap. Your school should be able to provide you with suitable headgear at first.

When you decide to buy a hat look for the British Standards kitemark and the numbers BS6473 or BS4472. The former replaced the old BS3686 and a great deal of rigorous testing has gone into producing this new standard hat. The BS6473 is similar to the traditional velvet riding cap but with additional safety features. Never modify a hat, for instance by cutting off the safety harness, or the safety standard no longer applies.

The BS4472 is the standard for jockey skull caps and these caps are recommended for cross-country riding and racing. This is also the standard which the Pony Club has adopted for all its activities. The BS4472 is being reviewed and it is possible that some amendments may be introduced.

Safety is a prime requirement when riding — invest in a new standard or jockey skull cap (shown on left) which is far safer than the old style of hat (pictured right) with its flimsy elastic chin strap.

For expert help on choosing and fitting a hat, look for the saddlers which display the British Equestrian Trade Association (BETA) Hat Fitting Diploma. An assistant will then be able to use the knowledge and skill she gained from attending a special BETA course to ensure you buy the right hat for your purposes.

Never buy a second-hand hat — it is a false economy which could cost you more than money alone. You never know what crashing falls the previous owner may have sustained when wearing the hat, and such falls will have decreased the hat's ability to withstand the same degree of impact a second time. A hat should be discarded after a heavy fall or knock.

Footwear is equally important. Strong shoes with continuous soles and low heels are fine to start with, then as soon as possible after buying a hard hat invest in some long rubber riding boots or short ankle-length leather jodhpur boots. Do not ride in training shoes or shoes without heels as if your foot slips through the stirrup iron and you then fall, there would be a nasty accident.

A pair of gloves, either string, cotton or leather, will help prevent sore, rubbed hands. If it rains or your horse sweats, the reins soon become slippery and it is easier to keep a good contact with them if you wear gloves.

If after a few lessons you are hooked on horses, put jodhpurs on the shopping list. The problem with trousers other than jodhpurs is that they tend to crease under the knee so becoming rather uncomfortable. There's now a whole host of jodhpurs on the market, from budget ones to fashionable corduroy styles in a variety of colours.

Hacking and show jackets are not necessary items of kit until you have become proficient enough to take part in competitions or formal tests of your riding ability. However, you may like to invest in one of the many quilted jackets on offer which can double as a normal coat as well as providing extra warmth for riding lessons in the colder weather. Waterproof, waxed cotton jackets are also ideal, especially if your riding school has no indoor riding facilities.

THE HORSE

Even if your riding school has only a few horses you are bound to feel that you will never be able to know and recognize them all. Yet within a few weeks you'll be putting names to the various equine faces as they peer over stable doors.

You will also start to learn, probably without consciously realizing it, the colours, markings, breeds and heights of the school's horse population. Then there are all the points of the horse, that is where the horse's knees, elbows, hocks etc are, plus items of tack such as the saddle, bridle and any other equipment the horse may wear.

Just as humans come in all shapes and sizes, so do horses. There are animals with long backs, straight shoulders, turned out feet etc — all kinds of defects of conformation (breed and shape) which affect how the horse moves and how comfortable or otherwise the horse is to ride.

To give you an insight into this facet of the horse world, dip into the following selection of information. As you meet and ride more horses or start to think about having your own horse you may find yourself referring to this section more and more. Plus, of course, part of being a good rider is being an understanding horseman too.

Size

All horses and ponies are measured in hands, the measurement being a perpendicular line from the highest point of the withers to the ground. Each hand is equivalent to four inches and the height is expressed in hands and inches, eg 14 hands 2 inches. You will also see this written as 14.2hh. An animal under 14.2hh is known as a pony; over 14.2hh and the animal is a horse.

Points of the Horse

During your riding lessons and as you learn some of the practical skills involved with horses, such as tacking up (putting the saddle and bridle on the horse), then you'll hear some of the terms involved in describing a horse. Take a look at the diagram for some of the most common points of the horse.

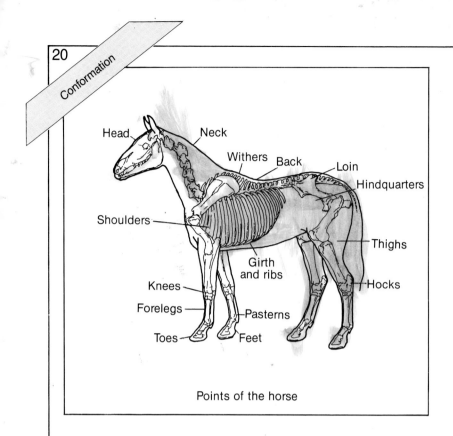

Points of the horse

Conformation

How a horse is put together, that is its shape and make, is important as it will affect how the horse moves and whether the animal is more susceptible to injury and disease. While the perfect horse does not exist, there are certain accepted good and bad points about a horse's structure and these are listed below. It is quite an interesting exercise to look at all the different types of animal in your riding school and see why some are more comfortable to ride than others: why some feel like armchairs whilst on others you appear to be sitting on a knife edge.

Head and neck

If a horse's head is out of proportion to the rest of its body then immediately the animal looks less attractive. As the horse's head and neck also act as a balancing pole, an overlarge head can put too much strain on the forehand.

The horse's eyes should be large, bright and with a good width between them indicating a kind temperament. The ears should be well placed and alert. A horse's neck should not be too heavy as the shape of the neck helps to determine how well the horse can carry his head.

Shoulders

These are especially important. If there is a good slope from the point of the shoulder to the withers then the horse will be a more comfortable ride. Short upright shoulders lead to short choppy strides. A greater slope means that the shoulders are better able to act as shock absorbers for the fore limbs when jumping, for example.

Back

As the rider's weight is supported by the horse's back, a reasonably short, strong back is preferable. This will enable the horse to move easily and efficiently, although if the back is too short the horse may over-reach and strike into his forelegs with his hind feet.

A horse with a slightly longer back can be more comfortable and faster than a short-coupled horse. However, if taken to extremes, a horse with a very long back will find it difficult to use his hindquarters properly.

Girth and ribs

A well-sprung rib cage, providing a large home for the horse's heart and lungs, is preferable to a shallow-girthed animal.

Hindquarters

The loin is the vital link between the horse's quarters, where all the propulsive power originates, and the horse's trunk. Therefore the loin needs to be strong and, as it is the least supported part of the back, short.

The hindquarters are the horse's 'engine room'. They should be strong, well-muscled and reach well down into the second thighs.

Legs

Have a look at a horse from the front. Does it appear that both forelegs are coming 'out of the same hole'? If so, this means that the horse is narrow-chested so not only is the chest cavity restricted but also as the horse's forelegs are close together the horse is likely to brush or knock them.

Knees should be broad and flat. The cannon bone, which is just below the knee, gives an indication of the horse's weight carrying capacity. A horse's 'bone' is measured at the widest part of the cannon, and you would expect a middleweight hunter to have about nine inches of bone.

Gently sloping pasterns are preferable to short upright ones as the pasterns act as shock absorbers; too much or insufficient slope means that the buffer effect is reduced and so the joints then have to take the concussion.

A horse's hocks are very important as the more flexible the hock the better able the horse will be to use his hindlegs to maximum effect, bringing them well under the body.

There's an old saying of 'No foot, no horse' — the horse's feet should be carefully looked after. They should be a good round shape, not too flat and wide nor too boxy and upright. The front feet should be a pair, as should the hind feet, with toes neither turning in nor out.

All in all, it's the overall general impression of the horse — he should look a well-proportioned and pleasing whole. The better proportioned he is, the easier it will be for him to do his job.

For new riders, it's also important that the horse they ride has a good sensible temperament and is a willing animal who will look after his rider.

Breeds

There are many different breeds of horses and ponies from countries all over the world. Britain has nine native breeds of ponies, ranging from the tiny Shetland to the much larger Dales ponies. The remaining seven Mountain and Moorland breeds in Britain are New Forest, Connemara, Fell, Highland, Dartmoor, Exmoor and Welsh ponies.

Some of these breeds are very old; for instance, Exmoor ponies are recorded in the Domesday Book. As well as the pure bred ponies you will also find horses and ponies which are a crossing of breeds. For example, a Welsh cob mare may be mated with a Thoroughbred stallion to hopefully produce a foal which will grow bigger than pure-bred Welsh cobs and be faster.

As you learn to recognize the different qualities of Britain's breeds you will probably be able to see that certain animals at your riding school have, for instance, Connemara or Welsh blood in them. You may hear the phrase 'half-bred', which is used to describe an animal which has a Thoroughbred as one of its parents.

Each breed has its own Society with which owners can register their horses. The records kept by the Societies are called Stud Books. Markings which are given as preferred are those for which the particular Society has a preference. The following gives a little information about the principal breeds:

Arab

Arabs have had tremendous influence in the horse world, but the breed is perhaps best known for creating the English Thoroughbred. It was back in the seventeenth century that the Darley, Godolphin Arabian and the Byerley Turk were imported into England to become the foundation sires of the Thoroughbred.

An ancient breed, Arabs are believed to have been living in the Arabian peninsula as long ago as 5000 BC. Renowned for its speed, courage, stamina, intelligence and beauty, the Arab horse has spread worldwide. Arabs make good all-round riding horses.

Connemara

Natives of Ireland, Connemaras are now also bred in England and are exported to many parts of the world. They are very popular, versatile animals and are often crossed with Thorough-breds to produce successful competition horses.

Height varies from 13hh to 14.2hh and grey is the predominant colour, while blacks are more common than bays or browns. Deep, compact bodies with good sloping shoulders, quality heads and free action make them all-purpose riding and driving animals.

Dale

One of the heaviest of our natives, the Dale is bred on the eastern side of the Pennines in Northumberland, Durham and Yorkshire. They are noted for their sure-footedness and sensible temperaments and can often be found employed as trekking ponies. Dales are also good harness ponies.

Height is usually around 14.1hh and most Dales are black although dark brown or grey is also found.

Dartmoor

From the Devon moorland, this hardy breed make good children's ponies, but they are also strong enough to carry adults, even though they do not exceed 12.2hh.

Their good conformation and kind, reliable temperaments result in Dartmoors being welcomed as family ponies. The preferred colours are brown, bay and black.

Exmoor

Over on Exmoor lives one of our oldest breeds. These ponies are easily distinguished by their mealy muzzles and mealy coloured markings around their eyes.

Again this is a strong and hardy breed, capable of carrying adults as well as children, even though the Exmoor maximum height is 12.2hh for mares and 12.3hh for stallions. Colours are bay, brown and mousey dun. No white markings are allowed.

Fell

Closely related to the Dale, the Fell pony is smaller and lighter. Fells originate from the northern side of the Pennine range and the Lake District.

Compact, powerful bodies with good sloping shoulders make them useful riding ponies. They vary between 13hh and 14hh and can be black, dark brown, dark bay and grey.

Highland

From the Scottish Highlands and the Western Isles, these are the strongest of Britain's mountain and moorland ponies. They are very calm sensible ponies standing 13hh to 14.2hh and are extremely strong and versatile, so making popular family ponies.

Highlands should have powerful hindquarters, compact bodies, strong necks and well-carried, kind heads. They have very full manes and tails as protection against the icy winds and rain. They are predominantly grey in colour but also in shades of dun, black, brown and liver chestnut with silver mane and tail. Look for the characteristic dorsal stripe which many Highland ponies have in addition to the zebra markings on the inside of the forelegs.

Irish Draught

A breed which is growing in popularity as when crossed with Thoroughbreds some superb hunters and all-round riding animals are produced. Originally a light draught horse, these animals are naturally good jumpers with good shoulders, legs and a free action.

New Forest

If you have holidayed in the New Forest area of Hampshire you may have seen the ponies roaming the heather and poor pasture. This breed is not as distinctive as some of the other British breeds due to the variety of other breeds which have been used over many years to improve the New Forest ponies.

In common with other native breeds, they are very hardy ponies and are versatile animals. They should have long sloping shoulders, strong quarters, plenty of bone and be deep through the girth. Sizes range from 12hh to 14.2hh with any colour except piebald, skewbald and blue-eyed cream being recognized.

Shetland

The smallest of our breeds, originating from the Shetland Islands off the north coast of Scotland. The ponies, measuring 38–42 inches (i.e. 9.2–10.2hh, although Shetland ponies are usually measured in inches), used to be employed by the crofters as pack animals, to work the land and as a means of transport.

Now they have become popular as riding ponies for very small children. Shetlands can be any colour although black is the most favoured.

Thoroughbreds

Thoroughbred horses can be seen on the racetrack and at famous events like Badminton and Burghley. Some riding schools which are also top training and examination centres have a huge variety of horses including Thoroughbreds for clients to ride. Smaller schools may also have half-breds.

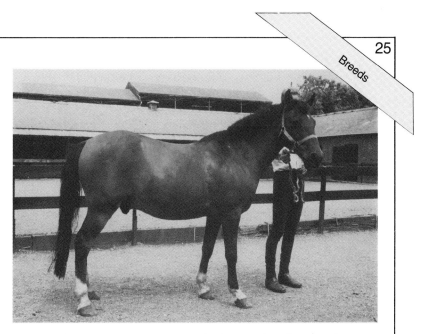

With the exception of the Arab horse, the Thoroughbred is acknowledged as having influenced more breeds than any other horse. It is also regarded as one of the most beautiful horses and Thoroughbreds have been successful in all kinds of equestrian sport.

Welsh

There is a Welsh mountain pony, Welsh pony, Welsh cob and Welsh

Above *Some coloured ponies have very distinguished and attractive markings.*

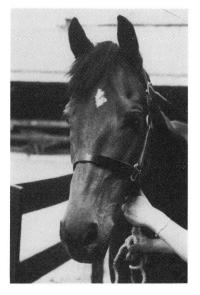

Right *Any small mark on a pony's forehead is called a star, irrespective of the shape of the mark.*

Sex

pony of cob type, with the Stud Book being split into various sections to accommodate the different types.

Welsh ponies are extremely popular, combining super looks, good temperaments and versatility, so appealing to a wide range of horse lovers.

Cob

This is a type of horse, not a breed, and is noted for its small head set on a strong neck, with a short, deep, compact body, short legs and good quarters. Cobs usually stand up to 15.2hh and are generally comfortable, sensible rides.

There are many more breeds and if you'd like more information write to the breed societies listed under Useful Addresses or consult one of the many books specifically on horse and pony breeds.

Sex

Mare A female horse or pony who is over four years of age.
Filly A young female horse or pony who is less than four years old.
Gelding A castrated male horse or pony.
Stallion An ungelded male horse or pony aged four years or over.
Colt An ungelded male horse or pony under the age of four years. Another term for ungelded is entire.
NB A foal is a young horse up to the age of 12 months. Then the animal is known as a yearling until he or she becomes a two-year-old.

Colours

People often have a preference for the colour of a horse, as well as its sex. There are several myths surrounding colour. For example, chestnut mares are generally associated with fiery temperaments although of course there are many cool-headed, sensible chestnut mares! Dun is the colour associated with the native or ancient breeds and some people prefer animals of this colour.

To determine the true colour of a horse you need to examine its points, ie its muzzle, tips of the ears, mane, tail and legs. For instance, a true black horse will have a black muzzle.

Foals do not necessarily stay the colour they are born, but by the age of two the adult colour has usually established itself.
Bay Horses may be dark or light bay depending on whether the colour of their coat is very dark brown or reddish-brown, but bays always have black points.
Black The horse has a black coat and black points with no other colour present except, perhaps, white markings on the face or legs.
Brown Along with black, bay and chestnut this is one of the four main horse colours. To establish whether a horse is brown or bay check its points carefully; if the mane, tails, legs etc are brown then the horse

is described as brown. It can of course have white markings such as a star, stripe etc.

Chestnuts A chestnut's colour is a bright reddish-brown but there are variations, such as light, dark and liver chestnut. The horse's mane and tail may be flaxen coloured, or slightly lighter or darker than the coat colour.

Dun The colour varies from a mousey colour to golden, but usually the horse has black points and there may be 'zebra' marks on the legs and a dorsal stripe.

Grey White is not a colour, it merely shows a lack of pigmentation. Grey is the result of pigmentation failure or variation and there are several types of grey. Where white and black hairs occur throughout the coat, the horse is known as a grey. If the black hairs are more pronounced, the horse is described as an iron grey. Conversely, a light grey is where the white hairs in the coat predominate.

Some animals are referred to as flea-bitten greys, because the dark hairs in the coat appear in tufts. As they grow older so the coats of grey horses grow whiter, but it is not correct to refer to a horse as being white. However, you may see an albino which has a white coat, pink rather than grey skin and usually pale-blue eyes.

Roan A mixture of two hair colours in the coat produces a roan. For instance chestnut and white hairs throughout a horse's coat give a strawberry roan; a bay roan is a combination of bay and white hairs, while black and white hairs throughout the coat give a blue roan.

Piebald A horse whose coat shows large, irregular but well defined patches of black and white.

Skewbald The horse's coat is made up of large irregular patches of white plus any other colour except black.

If you hear someone say that a particular horse is green, it has nothing to do with the animal's colour! It is a term used to describe a young, inexperienced horse.

Markings

A horse's markings can be very confusing but knowing your socks from your stockings can help you recognize the various horses at your riding school.

Star A white mark on the forehead, no matter what shape it is.

Stripe A narrow white line running down the face.

Blaze A broad band of white extending down the face and over the bones of the nose.

White face If the white extends over the forehead, eyes, nose and part of the muzzle then the horse is said to have a white face.

Snip Small white mark between or on one or the other of the nostrils.

Wall eye When the colouring of the iris is white or blue-white.

Legs Markings on the legs are usually named according to the part of the anatomy they cover; eg white heels, fetlocks or pasterns.

Stocking White extending right up the leg is known as a full stocking whereas white up to the knee or hock is just a stocking.

Socks White extending to half way up the cannon bones.

Ermine Used to describe black spots which appear on white markings.

Freeze-marking A man-made marking which can be seen on the shoulder or saddle patch of a horse. As horse owners are becoming more aware of the dangers from horse thieves so more animals are being freeze-marked.

This involves the horse being marked with three numbers and a letter. As the marking irons are applied to the skin the pigment is killed and the hair then grows back white in the shape of the appropriate number and letter. National records are kept of all marked horses and at the time of writing no horse freeze-marked by Premier Farmkey, who pioneered the scheme, has been lost to thieves.

White hairs You may see some horses with patches of white hair perhaps in the saddle or wither area. Often these are signs of an old injury or scar.

Understanding horses

People who have little to do with horses tend to regard them as huge, unpredictable creatures of little intelligence who are also dangerous at both ends! As any horse addict will tell you horses deserve a far better image than that. As a newcomer to riding and the horsey world, you'll be doing yourself, and any horse you ride, a favour if you take time to understand how a horse ticks.

Too often people make the mistake of assuming that animals think, reason and see the world in much the same way as we do. The sooner you can appreciate life from a horse's view, the quicker your riding will progress.

Think of the first horses way back in history. They were small creatures the size of a fox, with four toes. Over centuries they evolved into the magnificent creatures we know today, but along the evolutionary path they have retained the instincts which ensured survival of the first horses.

For modern horses' ancestors there was the ever present threat of predators, so they lived in herds for security and immediately there was any danger they fled. Anything landing on an early horse's back meant trouble, so his defence was to get rid of it by bucking or rearing. Other defence mechanisms were kicking, biting, stamping and lashing out with a foot.

Then along came Man who domesticated the horse, using it first as a pack animal, then as a means of transport for himself. The horse learnt to accept weight on his back and to obey the commands of a rider or driver.

Yet despite all the changes we can still see a horse's ancestry and instincts in evidence. Watch a group of animals living out at grass; one horse is usually boss of the herd and there's a pecking order for the rest. As a riding school pupil you are bound to experience the horse who just does not want to leave the rest of the group, which is its basic instinct that there is safety in numbers. For stabled horses their stable represents the security which the herd used to offer.

Stay around a stable yard for a while and watch how some animals object to hosepipes. As far as the horse's owner is concerned, she is simply hosing down the animal's legs but the horse who is unused to such procedure is highly suspicious. How is he supposed to know that the hose is not a snake?

Take the example of the young horse turned out in a paddock adjoining a railway line for the first time. The instant a train whizzes past the youngster zooms off in the opposite direction.

There are countless examples of the modern horse reacting to new experiences by employing his natural defences. Yet with training and sympathetic, firm handling the young horse becomes a well-behaved obedient riding animal. All we need now is a thinking rider to match with the horse.

FIRST LESSONS

On your first riding lesson you ought to be given some tips on approaching and handling horses sensibly. Before you even get on a horse it is helpful if your instructor introduces you to your mount.

Notice how horsey people approach their animals — they speak to the horse. Speaking as you approach the horse's stable lets him know that someone is on the way, while walking up to the horse from the side gives him the best chance of seeing you. Once again it is a case of realizing that the horse is different from you.

A horse has good eyesight but its range is very different from ours. With eyes placed on the side of his head it is possible for the horse to see a large area to the front, to the side and, to a certain extent, to the rear. His blind spots are straight in front of his face and immediately behind him. You may need to pass behind a horse to reach another stable or horse. If this is the case, it is even more important that you speak to him since he cannot see you, so any sudden movement behind him could spark off a natural reaction, a kick.

Horses are much more sensitive to the tone of voice you are using than to the actual words, and if you are nervous or frightened they will sense it and wonder what is wrong. If you are feeling apprehensive about a first lesson ask the instructor to spend time with you, taking you round the horse, letting you pat him and so on, so that you can make friends. With riding you are aiming to become a partnership so you may as well overcome any initial hesitation about your new partner.

Riding terms

During your introduction to riding and particularly when you join a class ride for the first time, you will discover that horsey people have their own 'language'. Some of these terms are self-evident but others can be puzzling to a new rider so several of the most common terms are listed below. Do not try to memorize them all before you start — they are included here so that you can feel more at home in your early lessons.

Ride The people and horses in a lesson.

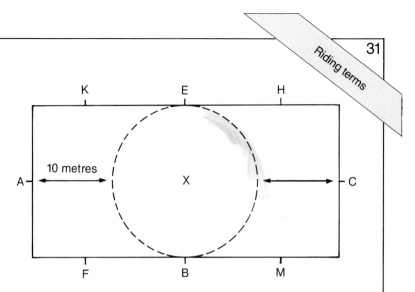

Manège The riding arena which is marked out with a set of letters in a universally accepted order.

Track The course you take as you ride around the manège, usually just inside the markers. This particular course is also referred to as the outside track. The inside track is the course which is about five feet away from the markers.

Leading file The person who is at the head of the ride and is responsible for ensuring that the pace of the ride is not too fast or too slow.

Rear file The rider at the back of the ride.

Right/left rein When you are riding around the manège in a clockwise or right-handed direction you are on the right rein. If you are moving in an anti-clockwise or left-handed direction you are on the left rein. When executing movements, the ride stays on the same rein unless instructed otherwise.

Change the rein Change direction. There are several ways of doing this; the most common ones are 'across the diagonal' and 'down the centre line'.

Distance For safety reasons you need to keep a sensible distance between you and the horse in front. This applies whether you are riding in the manège, to and from the arena or along bridleways etc. This distance is about four feet or 'half a horse's length'. Sometimes instructors will ask you to ride in open order whereby the distance between the horses is greater.

Correct your distance You should automatically ensure that the distance between you and the horse in front is about 'half a horse's length'. If you are too far behind make up the ground by cutting across a corner as you next approach a short end of the manège.

Whole ride walk on/trot/halt etc Each member of the class performs the exercise at the same time.

In succession Riders perform an exercise one at a time. The instructor

Here you can see a pony bending correctly around a circle. His hind feet are following in exactly the same track as the fore feet and his neck is gently flexed to the inside.

will say whether she wishes the leading or the rear file to commence the exercise.

Going large After performing a movement the ride rejoins the outside track and continues on around the school.

Transitions Change of pace. Transitions can be progressive, ie from walk through trot to canter, or acute, ie from walk to canter.

Leading a horse

Once you are happy approaching and patting the horse you may be asked to lead the horse to the manège for your lesson. Your mount should be tacked up with his saddle and bridle, plus any extra tack such as lungeing gear and protective boots if your first lesson is on the lunge.

A horse has two sides. As you stand alongside a horse facing in the direction of his head you are on his near or left side. A horse's right side is known as his offside. To lead a horse you stand on his nearside, positioned slightly in front of his shoulder.

If you are leading a bridled horse take the reins over his head and hold them in your right hand about five inches away from the bit. With your left hand hold the slack of the reins so they do not drag on the floor. Alternatively, fold up the bottom half of the reins and take hold of them with the right hand, the left hand holding the looped end of the reins lightly. It is important when leading that you do not let the reins or the lead rope drag on the floor where you or the horse may trip over them.

Look where you are going, say 'Walk on' to the horse and step forward. Make sure that you do not get too far behind as the horse walks on or that you are not too far in front and dragging the animal along. Take care to walk alongside and not directly in front of the animal where he may tread on you.

Above A workmanlike rider — note down the good points about his position and then test yourself by referring back to 'First lessons'.

Below By raising his hands and thrusting his lower legs back this rider has changed an effective riding position to an untidy and ineffective position.

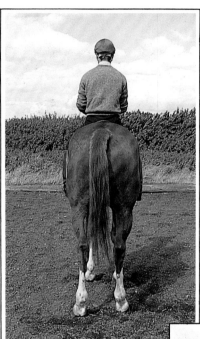

Left *Instructors often check your position from a back view to determine whether you are sitting square.*

Right *For many riders the most thrilling part of their sport — enjoying cross-country jumping.*

Below right *Over a sizeable but inviting show jump this rider is unfortunately leaning slightly to the right, but is otherwise nicely in harmony with the horse, allowing his mount sufficient freedom so that a good jump is produced.*

Right *You can see how this rider has collapsed to one side so pushing his whole body out of alignment.*

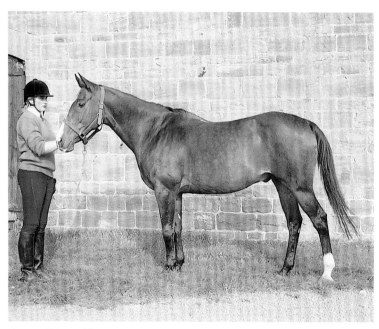

Above *This is a fine thoroughbred . . .*

Below *. . . but is happy to be with a pony of native blood, in spite of their different ancestry.*

Right Be positive and confident when leading a pony — if you are at all nervous your feelings will be transmitted to the animal.

Left Pre-ride checks: you can adjust your stirrups to the approximate length for you before you mount.

Right Fastening the girth too tightly will result in a sore pony. Use this test to determine whether your girth is correctly fastened, **but** remember to check the girth again once mounted.

Your instructor should be on hand to oversee the exercise and help if necessary. As you leave the stable and go through doorways etc, check that you are giving the horse enough room at either side so that he does not knock his shoulders or hips. Do not try any tight turns either — remember the horse has a longer body to manoeuvre than you.

Mounting and dismounting

Once safely in the manège your instructor will ask you to take the horse into the centre of the school and halt. This is so that you will be out

Left Mounting need not be a scramble, accompanied by a great deal of huffing and puffing! Stand close to the pony's front feet, with the reins gathered up to discourage the pony from wandering off.

Right Raising your foot high enough to place into the stirrup often causes a problem — if you are experiencing difficulties, let the stirrup down a hole.

of the way of anyone else and you can mount safely.

Before this step though, there are a few checks to do. After leading, your reins should be placed over the horse's head again, the girth, which holds the saddle in place, has to be checked and tightened if necessary, and finally the stirrups need to be altered for you. Watch how the instructor does all this, because it will not be long before you will be sorting this out for yourself.

Girths are usually tightened on the nearside. Raise the saddle flap to reveal the girth straps and guard. As the girth will probably be slack

Right You need to spring off your right leg — practice certainly makes perfect!

Below Do not pull on the saddle as you mount. People often hold on to the cantle, but this can damage the saddle, twisting the tree or framework upon which it is built.

Spring up . . .

. . . and gently lift your leg over the pony's quarters without giving him an unwanted kick.

Softly lower yourself into the saddle, ensure you have both stirrups, take up the reins and you are ready.

you need to tighten it one hole at a time; if you try to do it any faster you may pinch the horse and next time he could make the job more difficult by blowing himself out. Both straps should be level and your girth is fine when you can just slip your fingers in between the girth and the horse's belly. If it is too tight it will rub the horse and make him sore.

To check your stirrup length place the fingertips of your right hand against the stirrup bar and measure the stirrup against the length of your outstretched arm. The bottom of the stirrup iron should just rest in your armpit.

Now check that your hat is secure and you are ready to mount. Face the horse's nearside shoulder and take the reins in your left hand, steadying yourself using the horse's neck if you need to. Now turn your body slightly so that you are facing the horse's rear. With your right hand take hold of the stirrup iron and turn it towards you with a slight clockwise movement. Lift your left leg and place your foot in the stirrup. Grasp the seat of the saddle on the offside with your right hand and by springing off your right leg you should be able to transfer your weight into the left stirrup and swing your right leg over the horse's quarters. Be careful not to land heavily in the saddle.

Quite a few people find the initial process of mounting difficult and you won't be the first to receive a helping shove from the instructor! The only consolation is that it does become easier with time.

Dismounting is much easier. Take both feet out of the stirrups, lean forwards slightly, placing your left hand on the horse's neck and your right hand on the saddle pommel. Then swing your right leg up, back and over the horse's quarters so that you can vault off the horse. Be careful not to catch the horse's quarters as your right leg moves over the horse, and try to land on your toes. Make sure that you do not fall backwards as you land.

Once you are on board the horse, settle yourself so that you are sitting in the deepest part of the saddle, put your feet in both stirrups and let your instructor check your girth and stirrup length again. She will then show you how to hold the reins.

As the reins are lying on the horse's neck reach out with the knuckles of your hands facing upwards, take hold of the reins and then turn your hands so that your thumbs are uppermost and your fingers are curled in a half clenched fist. Move your little finger so that the reins from the horse's bit pass between your little finger and your third finger. The rein then comes up and over your index finger and is held lightly in position by your thumb.

On the move

Now for the moment of truth — you are about to move. If you are on the lunge your instructor has control of the horse so you don't have to worry about steering, just concentrate on yourself.

Quit both stirrups for dismounting, keeping a light contact on the reins.

Beginners tend to do one of two things when a horse first moves off; they either lurch forwards or slump backwards. You know what it is like standing on a crowded bus or tube train when the vehicle moves off and how you brace yourself to try and avoid being thrown around. Don't anticipate the horse's movement by leaning forwards, but just

Take both reins in your right hand and rest your left hand on the pommel. Lean forwards slightly and then swing your right leg up and over the saddle.

Your landing can be softened just by bending your knees a little. Aim to land by the pony's shoulder.

think of sitting in the saddle, rather than on the saddle, of sitting tall and still, and keeping your balance as the horse moves off.

Try to relax and feel the horse moving under you. If you tense up you will feel much more uncomfortable. You may feel as if you're rocking about, and there is no harm in slipping a finger under the neckstrap or saddle pommel to steady yourself, but don't try to use the reins to balance yourself, as any pulls on the reins will be felt by the horse as great jerks in his mouth.

As you are walking around, becoming accustomed to the horse's movement, your instructor will probably comment on your position. Don't get in a flap if it seems that you cannot do one thing without something else going wrong. It takes quite a time to be able to sit in the correct position, but having mastered it you'll be in the best possible place to give instructions to the horse and to be in balance and harmony with him.

The rider's position

How you sit on a horse is extremely important, because it can lighten the load for your mount or make it more difficult for him to move freely whilst carrying you. It is similar to giving a child a piggy back; if the child wriggles around it makes carrying the extra weight so much more difficult than if the child stays still. Imagine then how much easier it is for the horse if the rider is steady in the saddle, relaxed, supple and in balance with him.

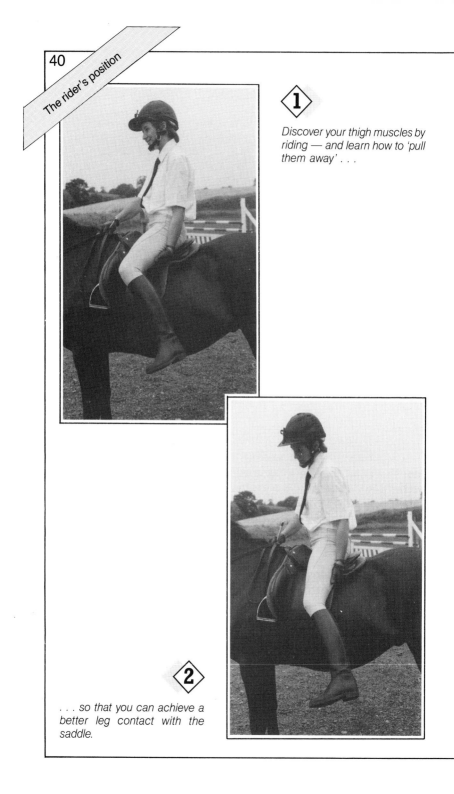

1

Discover your thigh muscles by riding — and learn how to 'pull them away' . . .

2

. . . so that you can achieve a better leg contact with the saddle.

One of the biggest obstacles to achieving a good riding position is tension. If you can concentrate on relaxing while on the horse you'll find it much easier to become an effective rider. Riding involves a combination of skills — balance, rhythm, co-ordination, accuracy and smoothness with minimum effort for maximum effect.

You have probably seen some of the top riders in action and thought they look tall, elegant and at one with their horses, and that they appear to achieve a great deal without actually doing anything. Of course they are giving very precise instructions to their horses but without it being obvious. All this takes a great deal of time and practice but from day one as a rider you can work towards this goal.

Most modern saddles are designed to give the rider every chance of sitting correctly in the central, deepest part of the saddle. To ride the horse to his best advantage you need to be able to feel what is happening so you must keep in contact with the saddle. To ensure a good even contact sit with your weight equally divided between your two seat bones, with the whole width of your seat resting on the saddle.

For those of you who are not too sure whether you are sitting on your seat bones try this exercise at the halt, while your instructor is holding your horse. Take both feet out of the stirrups and hold on to the pommel for extra security. Without tipping forwards or leaning back too much, lift up your legs so that your knees touch a few inches above the saddle. You should now be able to feel your seat bones. Hold for a few seconds and then relax, allowing your legs to hang down by your horse's sides again.

Every time you are in the saddle make a conscious effort to sit on your seat bones as this will give you a more stable position and you will be balanced quite naturally without any undue effort from you. Be careful not to shuffle backwards so that your bottom is on the cantle of the saddle, and beware of tipping forwards on to your fork.

Sit tall in the saddle but without forcing yourself and making your back stiff. You need to absorb the horse's movement through your back and hips so it is important that your back is upright and supple. If your back is rounded or hollowed, any movement by the horse will have a jarring effect upon you, so adding to the tension and creating a vicious circle of further tension and inability to absorb the horse's movements.

To help you sit tall, carry your shoulders, chest and head. Look where you are going, imagine that you have a chest adorned with medals and keep your shoulders back and level. Now try something very simple and you will see just how easily your position can be affected. Instead of looking straight ahead through your horse's ears, tilt your head forward and look down at his shoulder. As you do this your shoulders round, your rib-cage becomes depressed and your pelvis cramped. Because of this you cannot hope to absorb any movement by the horse properly and you will never be able to be in balance with him.

Exercises on horseback are beneficial at all stages of your riding career.

So, sit tall and make sure you are sitting level and square too. A common tendency is to collapse one hip which naturally affects your balance and throws your seat out of alignment with the horse.

Your arms should hang by and touch your sides, with the elbows bent. Imagine that there is a weight at your elbow. When seen from the side there should be a straight line from the horse's mouth, through the reins to the rider's elbow. Try not to clamp your arms into position as this will only make you stiff and tense.

Any stiffness in your shoulders, arms or hands will be transmitted to the horse's mouth via the reins. A horse's mouth is very sensitive and so riders need to have good, sympathetic hands which can give and take, be soft and supple. The reins are not there for the rider to use as a balancing aid — any pull on the reins will be felt as a harsh and unnecessary jerk in the mouth by the horse.

Your hands should be held level about three inches apart above the horse's withers. Crossing your hands over the neck will only confuse the signals you are sending to the horse. Be careful not to rest your hands on the horse's neck or move them about, but keep them steady and sensitive.

Stretch your legs down and around the horse. If your stirrups have been correctly adjusted you should feel comfortable. If they are too long you will be reaching for them, too short and you will probably feel as if you are perched on the saddle. Your knees should be slightly bent.

You can get an idea of what your riding position will feel like by this simple exercise off the horse. Stand with your feet about 20 inches apart, bend your knees slightly and gently bounce so that you can feel your knee and ankle joints absorbing the movement.

Your knees ought to be lying loosely against the saddle. Don't grip as this will produce tension throughout your leg. Make sure your knees are not turned off the saddle as this will affect the whole of your leg position, turning your calves so that you are 'cuddling' the sides of the horse.

If your thighs are rather well-endowed you may find it difficult to let your leg lie flat against the saddle, but all you need to do is take hold of the fleshy thigh muscle and pull it away from the saddle.

Your lower legs will be in contact with the horse's sides, again without any excess tension. Try not to turn your toes inwards or outwards too much. Either of these will affect the position of your lower leg. Check that your stirrup leathers are perpendicular to the ground — if they are not there is a fault in your leg position.

Another check for your position is that there should be an imaginary straight line going from your ear, through your shoulder, hip and heel to the ground.

The ball of your foot should be resting on the stirrup iron and your heels should be slightly lower than your toes. You'll probably be told 'heels down' on several occasions, but do not push them too far and exaggerate the position or you will create stiffness in your ankle joints. Your ankles and knees should act as shock absorbers.

Exercises on the lunge

To help you gain confidence and to work towards improving your position and suppleness your instructor will ask you to carry out certain exercises on the lunge. Some of these will be similar to the ones you have practised on the ground if you followed the pre-riding advice. You will not do all these exercises in one lesson, and some you will find easy to do whereas others will need to be worked towards as they require more confidence and a better sense of balance.

Lunge lessons are tiring for you and the horse, so they will only last about thirty minutes. How quickly people come off the lunge and join a beginners' lesson varies as everyone has their own learning pace. Once the instructor is happy that you have a reasonable seat, can stay in balance without hanging on to the reins and are safe, you will be moved on. To reach this point could take six lunge lessons or 12 — try not to be too anxious to progress more quickly. It is very important that a sound base is laid for the rest of your riding career, whether you wish to hack around the countryside or compete. If you take short cuts now you will only have to spend more time later establishing a good seat and correcting bad habits.

Your exercises on the lunge could include any or all of the following.

Arm circling

Take the reins in one hand, lift the other arm up and in front of you, then slowly bring it up and back so that a full circle is described. Be careful to keep the rest of your body relatively still — no tilting of your trunk! You should be able to feel your shoulder loosening up as well as your body stretching. Repeat with the other arm and then both arms together.

Shoulder hunches

A good tip for relaxing your shoulders is to hunch them up as if you are trying to touch your ears and then let them drop.

Touching the horse's ears

This will demonstrate how other parts of your body do move when you do not want them to! Lean forward and with outstretched arms gently touch the horse's ears. (NB Not all horses like their ears being touched, so do not try this unless the instructor asks you to.) Notice how your lower legs have swung back. Now try the exercise again but keeping your legs in position. You can also vary this by turning slightly to the side and with one hand touching the top of the horse's tail.

Touching toes

This helps to increase suppleness and is another exercise working towards independent use of the various parts of the body. Stretch your right arm upwards and then fold your body from the hips bringing your right arm down to touch your right toe. Repeat with the left arm. Then carry out the exercise reaching down with both arms at the same time. Another variation is to touch the right toe with the left hand.

Trunk twisting

This is good for loosening up the waist and hips region. Hold your arms outstretched to either side and gently swivel your body first to the left, then to the right. Do not look down as you perform this exercise.

Leg swings

With your feet out of the stirrups gently swing your legs, first one at a time and then together, backwards and forwards. You must be careful not to catch your horse by mistake. Keep the upper body relaxed and sit tall.

Ankle circling

Take your feet out of the stirrups and then rotate your ankles so that

Toe touching is useful for improving suppleness, balance and confidence.

you are describing a small circle. Your ankles act as shock absorbers so the more supple and tension free they are, the better.

While all these exercises are being carried out at the walk and halt you will be gaining confidence in the horse and yourself without even realizing it. You will also become accustomed to the feel of a horse in motion.

Trotting

When it is time for you to trot on a horse your instructor will teach you how to sit and rise to the movement. At first, sitting trot will feel very bouncy and you'll probably tense up so making it feel much worse. The secret is to relax and let your lower back and seat absorb all the bounces. Slip your fingers under the neck strap or saddle pommel to give yourself added security and think of 'soaking up' the movement of the trot in your lower back. Being able to stay in balance during sitting trot takes a great deal of time and practice, but as your body becomes more supple and tuned for riding you will learn the art of relaxing and sitting trot will become much easier.

To beginners, rising trot is a blessing after the discomfort of sitting trot but it can be just as difficult to master. This is because most riders make too much effort. They try to pull themselves up using the reins when in fact the horse's movement can be used to help the rider rise.

The trot is a two-time movement, ie one pair of diagonal legs moves in unison followed by the other pair of diagonal legs. In between there is a short period of suspension. All this adds up to an up and down as well as a forward movement. As you tried to sit to the trot you will have felt the up and down movement, so now sit and say to yourself, 'Up, down, up, down'. As you say up, stand on your stirrups, ie rise for one beat, and then sit for the down or second beat.

You will find it easier if you continue to say 'up, down' to yourself in rhythm with the horse's movement. Think of the rising movement coming from the thrust of the horse's back and from your legs and seat — you are moving up and forwards, **not** pulling yourself up using your hands.

To help to achieve this a good exercise on the lunge is to rise to the trot but without holding on to the reins. Let your hands hang down by your sides, place them on your hips or hold them in position as if you have imaginary reins. You will soon see that you can balance and rise without resorting to the reins.

Remember that in these first lunge lessons you will just be gaining the foundation blocks on which a firm independent seat will be built. As your riding progresses there will be times when you will return to lunge lessons. Riders of all standards can benefit as lungeing can improve a rider's seat and feel for the horse, help restore lost confidence, be used to correct positional problems and so on.

COMMUNICATION

During your early lessons the instructor will feed you with information about the aids or signals by which we let a horse know what we wish him to do. There are two types: natural aids, eg seat, weight, legs, hands, voice and thought, and artificial aids, eg whips, spurs, martingales and other gadgets.

For the moment we will concentrate on the natural aids. Although we will look at each separately, it is important to realize that they do not operate as separate entities. To ask a horse to do anything involves a co-ordinated application of all the aids.

It is a common belief among outsiders that the way to get a horse going is to give him a hefty kick in the ribs. A far better way of asking a horse to move off is to prepare to move, gather up the reins, think of sitting quietly but letting your body weight ease forward as the horse moves, close your legs around the horse and, as he moves forwards, allow with your hands, that is let your hands follow and yield to the movement of the horse's head.

Apart from being co-ordinated it is also important that your aids are clear. The horse will worry and wonder what is happening if a rider's legs are saying go but the rider is so tense he is hanging on to the reins signalling 'Don't you dare move'.

Do not under-estimate the power of a rider's will or the sensitivity of a horse. If you are determined to go past an unfamiliar object or hazard out on a hack, you will be riding positively and will achieve your objective. If, however, you are half-hearted about the exercise, or are frightened that the horse will take exception to the object and run off with you, then the horse will sense your fear and he will become worried too. Before you do anything, think and prepare — then you will give the horse the best opportunity of obeying you.

Natural aids

Seat and weight
Concentrate on achieving a balanced, firm, independent seat and everything else will follow in time. For instance, it is vital for your seat

to be good before you can be sure that your hands are not acting to the detriment of the horse.

How you use your weight is important, because you can 'steer' a horse using weight and leg aids alone. For an example of how your weight influences the horse, shift your weight on to the right seat bone. The horse will try to balance himself by moving to the right, ie to the rider's changed centre of gravity. Such a shift of weight would be virtually invisible to anyone watching the rider.Ultimately all riders should aim to appear to do very little while in fact communicating with their mounts a great deal.

Legs

In training a horse to understand the rider's aids, the best possible use is made of a horse's natural instincts. For instance, the horse moves away from the pressure exerted by the rider's legs.

By a sensitive use of his legs, a rider can create and control movement by the horse. It is the rider's lower leg which is the most effective and if used by the girth or just behind the girth the best response can be achieved. This is because it is here that the horse is very sensitive. A quick test will illustrate this. Stand next to a horse which is not saddled up and with your hand nudge the horse in the spot where a rider's leg, in the correct position, would give an aid. If you have located the correct spot, you should see a reflex action of the muscles.

When you are mounted you ought to be able to induce a response just by closing your legs around the horse's sides. Unfortunately, however, some riding school animals have experienced so many novice riders that they only respond to much heavier pressure from the rider's legs. You may see some riders swinging their legs back and kicking a horse's sides, but they are wasting their time as they are 'off target' anyway.

In addition to asking a horse to move forward, a rider's legs can also ask a horse to move sideways or can resist movement, eg stop the hindquarters swinging out.

Hands

Most people overdo the use of their hands, and they seem to forget that through the reins they have direct contact with the horse's mouth which is very sensitive and hopefully will remain so. All too often you see riders using too much hand and too little leg in their attempts to turn corners and so on.

Every movement you make with your hands should be done carefully and smoothly, from taking up the reins to asking for a change in direction or for a halt.

Through sensitive use of the hands you can guide a horse and control the movement which has been created via your leg aids. You need

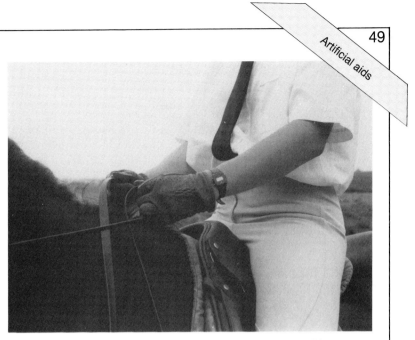

Sensitive, relaxed hands will be appreciated by any horse you ride.

to keep a firm, even contact on the reins but you must be ready to allow, eg when a horse walks he moves his head up and down so you must follow this movement. Your hands should also be able to resist, but it is better to think of this as not allowing rather than resisting, otherwise you may pull back on the reins. For instance, if you want to bring a horse back to halt from walk you would not pull on the reins; instead you would cease the allowing movement of your hands.

How can you tell whether your contact on the reins is sufficient? Hold the rein and imagine that you are holding a sparrow in your hand. You would need to be firm enough to prevent the bird from flying away but so strong that you would crush it. This is the type of feel or contact you need to keep on each rein.

Voice
Horses respond to the tone of the human voice and can be reassured, calmed, even reprimanded. Earlier there was an example of the importance of the rider's will — imagine in that instance how useful it would also have been to reassure the horse about the strange object using the voice.

New riders can also help themselves by using their voices, for example by saying 'Up, down' in time to the trot rhythm.

Artificial aids
Of the artificial aids, we will just look at whips and spurs.

Carry your whip so that it lies across your thigh, just above your knee.

Whip

A whip is used as a back-up to a natural aid. For example, a rider applies the aids correctly, but a horse refuses to walk on so the rider reinforces the leg aid by using the whip once behind his leg. This serves as a reminder to the horse.

Whips are also used as a punishment, but only more experienced riders should use them in this manner.

You will see many different whips in saddlers but basically the two which will concern you are the schooling whip, a long, thin whip measuring about thirty inches in length, and the much shorter, thicker jumping whip. The latter also has a flap of leather, sometimes called a paddle, on the end.

Whips are usually carried in the inside hand with the top of the whip against your thumb and the rest of the whip lying across your thigh, just above the knee.

To use a short whip you need to take your whip hand off the rein and apply the whip just behind your leg. As you change direction in the manège so you need to change over your whip. If you are carrying your whip in your right hand, take both reins into your right hand, with the left hand take hold of the whip top and pull it up until it is free of the right hand. Then return your left hand, with whip, to the normal position and take up the reins again.

Longer schooling whips are designed to be used without taking the whip hand off the rein and there is a different procedure for changing

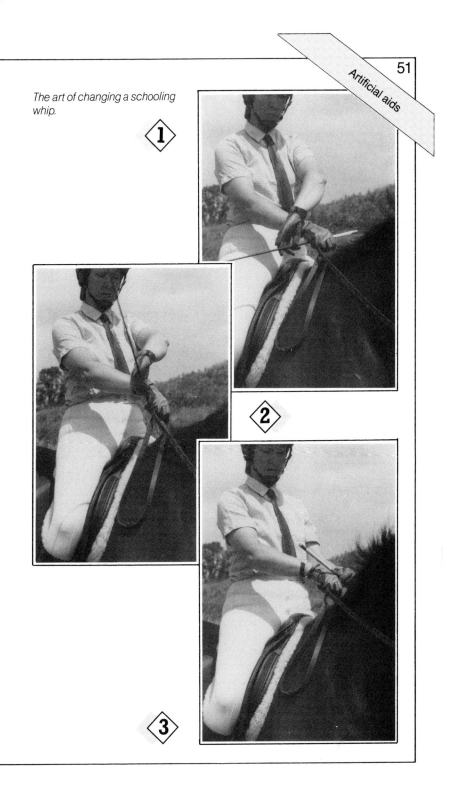

The art of changing a schooling whip.

over the whip. Owing to the whip length you would poke yourself in the eye and/or upset the horse if you tried to pull the whip through your hand.

If you are holding the whip in your left hand, take both reins in your left hand so your right hand is free to reach across and grasp the whip just below your left hand. Now turn the whip end up across your face and as it passes your nose let go with the left hand. The whip should now be in your right hand and you can take up both reins again.

Spurs

It may look good to wear spurs and they have their uses in reinforcing a rider's leg aids, but they should only be worn and used by riders who have complete control of their legs. Imagine the damage which could be done by a novice rider wearing spurs and flapping his legs about all over a horse's sides.

ON THE MOVE

Most of the time you will have spent on horseback so far will have been in walk and trot. These are two of the three basic paces of horses (although certain breeds have different gaits, eg the Tennessee Walking Horse has a gait which is half walk half run). The third basic pace of a horse is the canter, with the gallop being an extension of the canter. To help you as a rider it is useful to understand what happens to the horse in each pace. However, before looking at movement, let's start with the halt and see how a horse's static body position can affect the way he will move off.

In halt the horse should be standing square so that his weight is evenly distributed on all four legs. He ought to be paying attention to his rider so that as soon as a command is given the horse responds. It is rather like an athlete on the starting blocks; the one who is crouched down in the correct position is far more able to respond to the starting gun than the one who is still fiddling around, trying to get his feet comfortable on the blocks.

As you are sitting on a horse in halt try to sense whether he is standing square or not. It is fairly easy to tell whether one of the forelegs is too far forward, but it takes a little more practice to feel which hindleg is being left behind. A horse's power is generated by his hindquarters so you can see that if he is not standing properly then some of his 'engine' power will be lost.

The horse's paces explained

What happens as you ask a horse to move off into walk? The walk is a four-time pace, ie there are four even beats to every stride and the sequence is as follows:
1. Near-hind
2. Near-fore
3. Off-hind
4. Off-fore

The horse should swing along in a free easy rhythm of 1, 2, 3, 4 as each leg is lifted and put down separately. His strides should be

Above Walk is a four-time pace: here you can see the near-hind has come to the ground with the near-fore about to complete the second stage of the four-time movement.

Below Now the off-hind has come underneath the horse's body and the off-fore comes forward to finish the cycle.

even and unhurried but he should not be dragging his feet.
As he walks, the horse nods his head and the rider must allow
with his hands to follow this movement. If a rider restricts this
balancing movement by the horse then the animal could stumble
and it would not be able to walk out freely.

As your horse is walking around the manège try to feel the rhythm
of the hoofbeats; it helps if you count out 1, 2, 3, 4; 1, 2, 3, 4 in time
to the horse's movement. It is amazing how much you can feel if you
close your eyes for a short while, say just for the length of one side
of the school (do not try anything like this if there is no-one else around),
and call out 'Now, now' as the horse's left foreleg comes forward.

The walk is the easiest pace for a rider to maintain position. All the
paces have variations in them; in walk, for example, there is collected,
medium, extended and free walk, but for a novice rider's purposes work
is carried out in the most natural paces for the horse, ie medium walk,
working trot and working canter.

Trot is the second of the paces and has a two-time beat. When a
horse trots he moves his legs in diagonal pairs, the off-fore and near-
hind (right diagonal) together, and the near-fore and off-hind (left
diagonal) together. As he springs from one diagonal pair to the other
there is a moment of suspension. It is therefore not surprising that a
new rider finds the trot to be a rather bouncy pace and one in which
it is more difficult to maintain position.

In trot a horse's head remains virtually still so it is important that
the rider keeps his hands quiet too.

A rider may sit or rise to the trot. Hopefully your lunge lessons will
help you to achieve a reasonable sitting trot before you attempt rising
(also known as 'posting') to the trot.

In rising trot, you rise and sit on alternate diagonals as this makes
life easier for you and it saves the horse's back. Do not think of the
rising action as being a totally upward movement. Instead, as you rise
think of bringing your hips forwards towards the saddle pommel and
of barely leaving the saddle rather than making a huge effort. You do
not want to bring your body well out of the saddle.

If the rider is riding on the correct diagonal it is also easier for the
horse to balance himself — but what is the correct diagonal and how
do you check for it? If you are riding around the manège on the right
rein, ie moving clockwise, you need to be riding on the left diagonal,
that is the near-fore and off-hind. In order for the horse to support your
weight better and so that you can use your leg aids to the best
advantage, you should sit in the saddle as the left diagonal pair of legs
touch the ground. This means that you sit as the off-hind (which on
the right rein is the inside hind) comes to the ground.

Experienced riders have learnt how to feel whether they are on the
correct diagonal but fortunately for novice riders there is an easier
way to check. If you are correct, the horse's outside shoulder (that

Above In trot, a two-time pace, you can clearly see the two diagonals: here the left diagonal, ie near-fore and off-hind, are in action . . .

Below . . . closely followed by the right diagonal, ie off-fore and near-hind.

is the one nearest to the wall of the manège) will be coming back towards you as you sit.

To change diagonal the rider has to sit for an extra beat. When your instructor first covers diagonals in a lesson you will have the chance to practise changing and checking diagonals. Later on in your riding career, when you start to ride out in the countryside, remember to change diagonals at regular intervals so that the horse does not become tired or stiff on one side. In your class lessons remember that every time you change the rein you will need to change diagonals too.

One of the most exciting moments of your early riding career will be when you canter. This feels very different — a rolling sensation rather than the bumpy feel of the trot. Canter is a three-time pace with three beats followed by a moment of suspension.

Just as the trot has correct diagonals so the canter has correct leading legs. If you are cantering around the manège on the right rein then the sequence of legs would be:

1. Near-hind
2. Off-hind and near-fore together
3. Off-fore
4. Moment of suspension

This is canter with the right leg leading. You can check that the horse is on the correct leg by glancing down; you should be able to see the right foreleg coming forward. Don't tip forward to check the canter leading leg or you will unbalance the horse and could even make him stumble.

For a left canter lead, the sequence of legs would be:

1. Off-hind
2. Near-hind and off-fore together
3. Near-fore
4. Moment of suspension

In canter the horse's head and neck move so it is vital that your hands are sympathetic and allow for this movement. The rolling feel of the canter results from the horse's hindquarters rising as the leading foreleg hits the ground and then falling as during the moment of suspension the horse's head rises.

To be able to sit to the canter a rider needs a relaxed supple pelvis and hips. Some people become over-anxious when they canter so making their bodies tense with the result that they grip up with their legs, hang on by the reins and find it even more difficult to absorb the horse's movement. For your first canters there is no harm in holding on to the neckstrap or saddle pommel for extra security.

For the moment we will concentrate on these three paces — galloping and jumping come later.

Left *The easiest place to ask for a canter strike-off is in a corner, but you need to have the horse going forwards actively and listening to you. Here the rider is on the left rein and you can see the off hind is providing the propulsive force with the near hind and off foreleg, acting as a pair, about to provide the second stage of this three-time pace.*

Right *As the diagonal pair of legs comes to the ground so the near fore, which on the left canter is the leading leg, is about to be extended.*

Left *As the leading foreleg hits the ground the horse's hindquarters rise slightly. Before the whole sequence starts again there is a moment of suspension when the horse's head rises, hence the rolling feel of the canter.*

School movements

Once off the lunge your lessons will be spent improving your basic position and gaining confidence in riding the horse in a manège, carrying out various exercises. Let us first consider the schooling area in which you will be working.

Most manèges tend to be 40 × 20 metres (44 × 22 yards) and they are always marked in the same way. In the centre of the short side by which you enter the arena is the letter A and opposite this on the second short side is the letter C. The mid-points of the two long sides are marked by the letters B and E. At each end of the long sides, situated six metres in, are four markers K, H, M and F. These mark the diagonals across the school, as well as indicating the straight length of the long sides of the school. If you are turning a corner you can use these markers as a guide — do not start to turn until you have passed these points. The centre of the school is known as X but there is no visible marker.

Riding corners

Up to this point you have been able to leave the steering to the instructor, but now it is your turn to tell the horse exactly where to go. Most novices find that corners are the real bug-bears as the horses often insist on cutting across a corner, much to everyone's annoyance. So how do you ensure that the horse does use the corners of the school properly?

Think about your leg aids and the effects they have upon a horse. They create movement, make the horse use his hindlegs more effectively and let the horse know in which direction you wish to move.

Now back to the corner cutting problem. For our example you are riding on the right rein. As you approach the corner use your right leg by the girth to push the horse to the left and therefore on to the track you want to follow around the corner. Ensure that you are not leaning around the corner yourself as that will encourage the horse to fall in and cut the corner.

You must also check that your contact on both reins is even and that you ride firmly through the corner without allowing the horse to reduce or quicken his pace. You are aiming to get around the corner on a smooth curve with the horse's hindlegs following on the same track as his forelegs. You do not want the horse drifting or wandering from side to side.

In very basic terms your inside hand will be asking for direction while the outside hand will be regulating the pace and allowing the horse to flex to the inside. Your inside leg will be asking for energy and encouraging the horse to bend correctly from head to tail, with the outside leg preventing the quarters from swinging out.

A horse finds it very easy to bend his neck but it is much more difficult

Making full use of the school by riding into the corner.

for him to keep the rest of his body on a smooth curve around the corner. Therefore he may bend his neck but keep the rest of his body straight. As you ride around a corner or on a circle you should just be able to see the corner of the horse's inside eye — any more than that and the horse is bending his neck too much.

Faults often arise on corners because the rider's seat has slipped to one side so unbalancing the horse. Remember that you should be looking through the horse's ears to where you want to go, keeping your shoulders and hips parallel to the horse's shoulders and hips.

Do not cross your hands over the horse's neck in an effort to move the horse over. It will be easier at first if you practise riding corners at a walk, as you will have more time to co-ordinate your aids. Riding too deeply into a corner is just as much a problem as cutting across because you will not be able to achieve a smooth curve.

Changing the rein

There are numerous ways in which you can change the rein, that is, change your direction. Initially you will find yourself using a selection of the following methods:

a) Down the centre line, ie from C to A or vice versa. Whenever you turn it is vital that you maintain the rhythm of the pace and that the exercise has a smooth flowing execution. The key is to always think and prepare ahead — and look where you are going. Do not try to turn too sharply on to the centre line or you will find yourself overshooting the line anyway.

As the centre line itself is not actually marked you need to look at your destination and keep moving in a straight line towards the marker. Keeping a horse straight is not as easy as you might imagine but you will find it useful to think of the horse moving in a tunnel provided by your hands and legs.

b) From B to E and vice versa. Again it is important to prepare and look ahead so the turn is not too abrupt. Be careful not to tip your body in towards the centre of the arena or you will be 'motor biking' around the turn. Your outside leg needs to ensure that the horse's quarters do not swing out while the inside leg can keep the rhythm of the pace going.

c) Across the diagonal, ie from F to H and K to M. When riding on the right rein you would be able to change the rein across the diagonal from M to K or from K to M. However, if you tried to ride from H to F whilst on the right rein the turn needed at H would be too acute.

On the left rein you can turn easily from F to H and H to F but not across the K-M diagonal.

Twenty-metre circles

These circles involve using the complete width of the arena and they can start at A, C, B or E. The circles from A and C will both pass through X, the mid-point of the A-C centre line. They also touch the track about four metres in from the diagonal markers. Therefore K, H, M and F are not actually on any 20-metre circle. If the 20-metre circle starts at either B or E, its other two points are halfway between X and C, and X and A.

Make full use of the arena when riding circles and look around the circle, keeping the same distance from the centre of the circle all the way around; otherwise you have some very strange shaped 'circles'.

Be conscious of the position of your hands. Try not to let one drop lower than the other and beware of pulling the horse's head and neck to the inside. If you overdo the flexion to the inside you will only succeed in throwing the horse off balance. You should just be able to see the corner of the horse's inside eye.

Twenty metre circles can be ridden in trot and canter.

Figures of Eight

A good exercise for your co-ordination of aids is to join together two 20-metre circles so that you ride a figure of eight. Ride a 20-metre circle from A and on the second circuit, as you approach X, change the rein and complete another 20-metre circle passing through C.

As you change direction you need to alter your aids, eg you are on the right rein, on a 20-metre circle from A, so your inside (ie your right) leg is by the girth and the outside (your left) leg is slightly behind the girth. At X you will be straight for a horse's length before moving off on the left rein to complete a 20-metre circle at C. Your leg position will therefore have swopped over just before X so your right leg has now become the outside leg and your left leg has become the inside leg.

On the right rein your right hand was gently feeling the rein, with an action similar to squeezing water out of a sponge, so asking the horse to flex and now on the left rein, the left hand is performing this task.

Figures of eight can be ridden at trot and canter — with a canter exercise you come down to trot for a couple of strides through X before striking off again on the correct canter lead for the new direction.

Half circles

These make use of half 20-metre circles and can be linked together as a way of changing the rein. For instance, you ride from C to X as if you are riding a 20-metre circle from C, but at X you ride in a straight line for a horse's length and change the rein so that you are riding from X to A in another half circle.

Serpentines

Riding a three-loop serpentine is more difficult, demanding accuracy and good co-ordination of aids to ensure a flowing movement.

The exercise is started from either C or A with, for example, one loop from A to just slightly beyond K, cutting the centre line one-third of the way in from A, the second loop hitting the track at B and then cutting the centre line again two-thirds of the way along, before the third loop hits the track just before H to finish at C.

The loops are not perfect semi-circles but they must be equal. If you are carrying out the exercise in rising trot you need to change your diagonal every time you cross the centre line.

There are a great variety of school movements but even with this limited selection you can put together quite an interesting programme. Other exercises such are rear file overtaking ride and assuming position of leading file, leading file canter on to rear of ride, etc, test your control of the horse while plenty of transitions (ie changes of pace) will help you become accustomed to applying the aids.

It is only by riding that you will find your balance, learn how to co-ordinate your aids, develop an independent seat and a 'feel' for the horse's movement. All the time you will be overcoming small challenges, certain riding skills will start to become second nature and you will be enjoying your new hobby.

MAKING PROGRESS

As you become more familiar with the horses and people at your riding school you will probably want to become more involved, perhaps by tacking up your mount, turning the horses out after the last lesson of the day and so on. With growing confidence there is a lot you can do, both on and off horseback.

Tacking up

On your first attempt ask your instructor or another of the school's staff to oversee the procedure. Make sure you have the correct tack for the horse concerned — it is strange how people will insist on trying to put a pony bridle on to a huge horse when common sense ought to make them question whether they have made a mistake!

To carry a bridle it is easiest to slip it over your shoulder, with the headpiece and reins resting on your shoulder and your arm between the browband and noseband. Carry a saddle on your left arm with the pommel close to your elbow.

When you tack up, the bridle is put on before the saddle, so you therefore need to ensure that the saddle is out of harm's way whilst you bridle the horse. Place the saddle over the stable door, but make sure that the horse cannot push it off. If you have to put the saddle on the floor place it pommel down with the cantle leaning against a wall or door. You can use the girth to protect both the pommel and the cantle from scratches.

If the horse is secured by a head-collar, put the reins over his head before undoing the head-collar, removing it from the horse's head, slipping it around his neck and fastening it up again. This way the horse is never completely loose.

Some horses may throw up their heads and make bridling difficult, so stand alongside the horse's head on his nearside. Slip your right hand under his jaw and bring it round to the front of the animal's head. Grasp hold of the bridle, about halfway down the cheek pieces, with your right hand. With your left hand take hold of the bit and guide it into the horse's mouth. Most horses have been taught to open their mouths to accept the bit but if the horse is awkward you can easily

1

If you are asked to tack up it will probably be within the confines of the stable, but we moved outside for a clearer photograph. Reins over the pony's head is the first step.

2

This ensures that you still have some means of restraining the pony once the headcollar has been removed.

Above *A well-collected pony — horse and rider in perfect harmony.*

Below *Ready to start the lesson — this is a sensible size of class.*

Above left *Keeping a respectable distance between riders.*

Left *The class working in succession over one trotting pole as a preliminary exercise before jumping.*

Above *One at a time over several trotting poles followed by a small cross pole.*

Right *A badly-fitted drop noseband such as this will restrict the horse's breathing.*

Above *Take care when riding along country lanes, and make sure you know the Highway Code.*

Below *Always take the opportunity to become involved in the day-to-day stable yard duties, to complete your riding experience.*

By slipping your right hand under the pony's head and bringing your hand round, you can steady the pony and prevent him lifting his head up to make bridling difficult.

Once the bridle is on make the pony comfortable, by pulling the forelock from underneath the browband and checking that the browband is not touching the pony's ears.

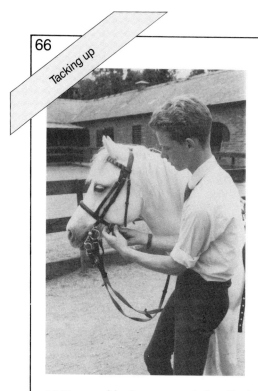

Fasten the throatlash and then the noseband.

encourage him to co-operate by slipping your thumb into the side of his mouth. There's a gap between his front teeth and the molars at the back of his mouth so you will not be bitten.

With the bit in the horse's mouth, bring up the bridle so that you can slip the headpiece over the offside ear first and then over the nearside ear. Pull the forelock out from underneath the browband, fasten the throat-lash and then the noseband. Replace the head-collar on top of the bridle if necessary.

The saddle is placed on the horse from the nearside. Check first that the stirrups are run up as if they are hanging loose they could hit the horse and startle him. The girth should be attached to the offside of the saddle and then folded over the seat.

Place the saddle on the horse's back but well up on the withers so that you can then slide it back into place. Do not try to slide a saddle forward into position as you will be moving against the lay of the coat and this can cause some discomfort for the horse.

Go round to the other side of the horse, check that the saddle flap isn't turned under, let the girth down and check that it is not twisted. Now return to the nearside and attach the girth, taking care not to pull up the girth too tightly or too quickly. Do not tighten the girth ready for riding until you are about to mount. To ensure that the horse's skin is not wrinkled by the girth (which could cause soreness) take hold of the horse's forelegs in turn and stretch them out forwards.

Above *Lift the saddle on to the pony's back using your right hand to prevent the numnah from folding over or creasing.*

Below *Slide the saddle into position, moving with the lie of the coat.*

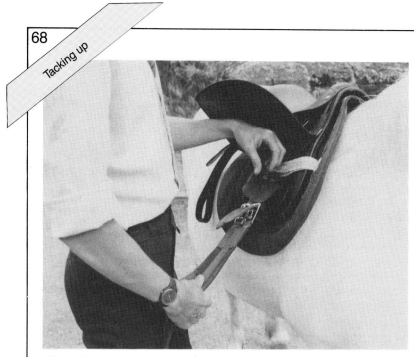

Above Move around to the other side to attach the girth and check that the numnah strap has been attached to the girth straps.

Below Return to the pony's nearside and bring the girth under the pony's belly so that it can be fastened. Check that the girth is not twisted.

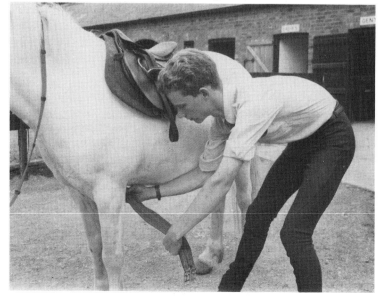

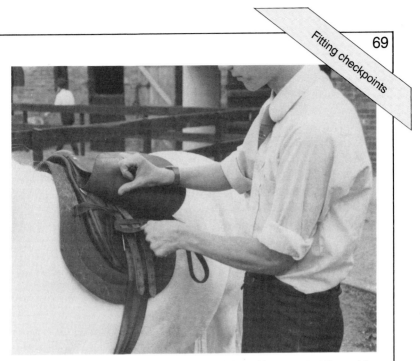

Girth guards should be pulled down over the girth buckles to protect the saddle.

If you have the correct tack for the horse then it should fit properly, but there is no harm in just checking the fitting as you tack up your various mounts because it will be good practice if you ever need to fit your own animal with tack.

Fitting checkpoints

Saddle
The pommel must not rest on the horse's withers as this would make the horse very sore. There should be a gap of at least three fingers' width between the withers and the saddle arch. Test that there is clearance when a rider is sitting in the saddle as well.

Horses vary in their build — some are very narrow chested whereas others are very broad — so there are different width fittings for saddles. Trying to squeeze a medium-sized horse into a very narrow saddle will only result in the horse being pinched on either side of the withers. It is important therefore that the saddle is of the correct width for the horse.

The length of the saddle is also important, for instance using a large horse saddle on a 14hh cobby pony could mean that the weight of the saddle and rider is being placed over the pony's loins, a weak part

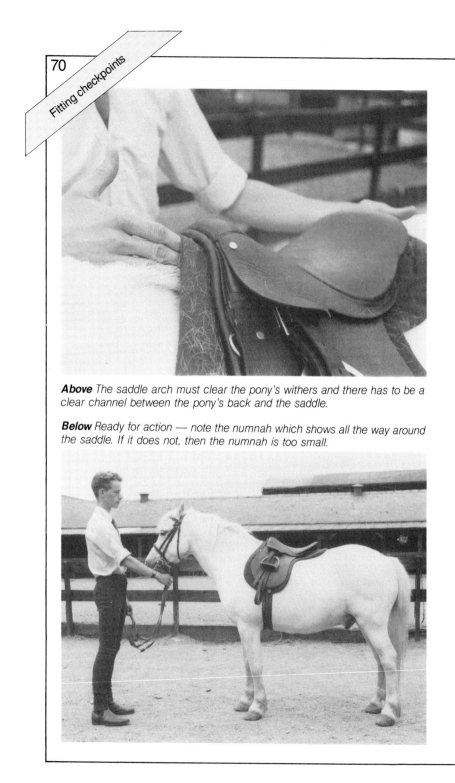

Above *The saddle arch must clear the pony's withers and there has to be a clear channel between the pony's back and the saddle.*

Below *Ready for action — note the numnah which shows all the way around the saddle. If it does not, then the numnah is too small.*

of his back. This would also prevent the pony from being able to get his hindlegs properly underneath him, so restricting his movement.

When the saddle is on the horse look along from the cantle to the pommel: there should be a clear channel along the backbone. Even with a rider in the saddle, there should still be no pressure on the horse's spine. The idea is that the saddle rests evenly on the horse's back so that the weight of the rider is distributed on either side of the backbone without any undue pressure.

If a saddle is in need of restuffing then it will not be able to fulfil the function of distributing the rider's weight evenly. Look at the panels of the saddle — are they flat? If a saddle is used in this condition it causes pressure on the horse's spine, resulting in soreness. Too much stuffing in the saddle panels can be just as much a problem as the saddle may rock and rub the horse's back.

In large yards saddle-shaped pads called numnahs are used to help keep the saddle clean, although a well-fitting saddle does not really need a numnah underneath it. If they are the correct size you will see about one inch showing all round under the saddle. Some people use them when show-jumping and cross-country jumping as extra protection: as a horse jumps he rounds his back so over larger fences it is possible that the spine may touch the gullet of the saddle, and using a numnah will help to prevent any contact being made.

Numnahs must be kept clean and should not be allowed to become hardened as this would cause friction on the horse's back. It is also important to ensure that the numnah is pulled well up into the saddle arch and the saddle gullet to ensure that no pressure is exerted on either the withers or the spine.

Bridles

The bit needs to be the correct width for the horse's mouth and should be resting high enough in his mouth so that the corners of his lips are just wrinkled. When the bit is held straight out across the horse's jaw there should be a gap of a quarter of an inch on either side of the mouthpiece. If the bit is too big or fitted too low the poor horse will have his teeth bashed by the metal bit. Too narrow a bit will cause soreness through pinching.

The browband should not be too tight or it will rub the horse's ears. Its purpose is to ensure that the headpiece, which should lie flat just behind the horse's ears, does not slip down the neck.

There is a throat-lash to stop the headpiece from slipping over the ears, but this needs to be fitted fairly loosely. Allow four fingers' width between the throat-lash and the horse's cheek.

Fitting a noseband is very important — cavesson nosebands are the most common and these should lie about two fingers' width below the projecting cheek bones. Allow for two fingers between the

Three quick pointers to a correctly fitted bridle.

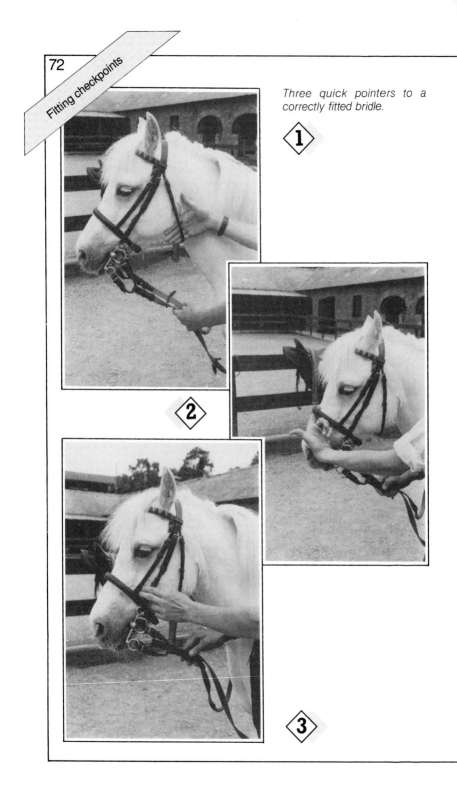

noseband and the horse's nose. Drop nosebands should lie well above the nostrils, allowing for the width of four fingers. If fitted incorrectly they can restrict a horse's breathing.

Martingale

If a martingale is worn it should be placed over the horse's neck with the reins. When saddling up the girth is put through the martingale loop which fits between the horse's front legs.

Tightening the girth when mounted

To do this, take both reins in your right hand and keep a good even contact so that the horse is not encouraged to move off, but if he does, you can quickly take corrective action. With your foot still in the stirrup, move your left leg forward and then with your left hand pull up the saddle flap. Hold on to the flap with your right hand so your left hand is free to reach for the girth strap and tighten the girth.

If you keep your forefinger close to the buckle pin you can guide it into the next hole more easily. Check that the girth has been tightened evenly on each strap.

Altering stirrups when mounted

Start with the nearside stirrup. Place your reins and whip into your right hand and keeping your foot in the stirrup, pull the buckle of the stirrup

Remember to keep your feet in the stirrups when tightening the girth.

Left Once aboard check your stirrup length by taking your feet out of the stirrups and letting your legs hang down in a relaxed manner. The bottom of the iron ought to be level with your ankle bone.

Below If you need to adjust the length place your feet back in the stirrups.

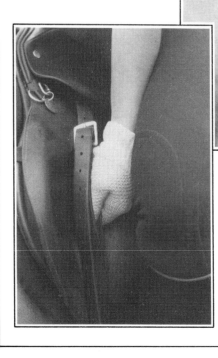

Left Remember to pull the buckle back up to the stirrup bar once you have altered the stirrup length.

leather away from the stirrup bar. Adjust to the required length, again keeping your finger close to the buckle so you can guide the pin into the correct hole easily.

Take hold of the underside of the stirrup leather and pull it down so that the buckle end of the leather returns to its correct position close to the stirrup bar. Adjust the other stirrup, then take up your reins again.

Untacking

The tacking up procedure is reversed, ie the saddle is removed first, followed by the bridle.

When a rider dismounts the girth should be loosened and stirrups run up. To remove a saddle, undo the girth on the nearside, removing from the martingale loop if necessary. Take hold of the saddle, left hand on the pommel and right hand on the cantle, and lift it off the horse's back. As the girth comes into view take hold of it with the right hand and place it over the saddle seat. To help stimulate circulation pat the horse's back in the saddle area.

Now for the bridle. Undo the noseband and throat-lash, take the reins, and martingale if worn, up to the headpiece and then gently remove the bridle. As you lower the bridle be careful that you do not let the bit bash against the horse's teeth. Do not be too hasty about lowering the bridle or you may catch the horse in the mouth.

Whenever you are carrying saddlery, try not to let any of the items drag on the floor.

You may find some horses wear protective boots on their legs. It is always wise to ask a member of the school staff to show you how to put these on as there are a wide variety of boots. If you need to remove any boots always rub the horse's legs where the boots have been to help circulation.

It is not sensible to leave a horse tacked up and loose in his box, because he could easily lie down or roll which would damage the saddle, an expensive item of equipment. For safety's sake always ensure that the reins are not left hanging loose where the horse could get caught in them or catch them on a stable fixture. Slip them behind a stirrup iron or pop them through the throat-lash.

Warming up a horse

As soon as all the riders in your class lesson have mastered the basics of controlling a horse and undertaking various exercises, your instructor may start to let you work your horses individually. This will be at the beginning of a lesson when you will have a few minutes to warm up your horse before forming a ride and carrying out the rest of your lesson.

You can use this time to loosen up your horse, get him going forwards willingly and listening to you. If the horse has been standing in his stable for the past couple of hours he will need the first few minutes of the lesson to be spent in walk and trot so that his muscles can be warmed up. The horse needs this limbering up period. After all, you wouldn't leap out of bed in the morning and go on a six-mile run without doing some warming up exercises first.

Make use of circles, transitions and changes of rein to wake up your horse, get his attention and to encourage him to work actively. You need to add variety to this riding in period — just going round and round on the same rein is boring for both horse and rider.

For trot work, rise rather than sit, as rising trot is easier on the horse's back at this early stage of the lesson. Just before the end of your riding in time give the horse a short canter on either rein to complete the loosening up process. After this you should be ready to tackle the rest of the lesson.

As you become more experienced your instructor may ask your opinion of the horse. Perhaps you felt that the horse was stiffer or more resistant on one rein? Was he a co-operative ride? If not, why not? How could you persuade him to put more effort into his work? Does the horse feel balanced? Did you experience any problems and if so, is there anything you would like to ask? Is the horse a short or long striding animal?

Think of these points as you are riding around and you will be better prepared to answer if your opinion is unexpectedly required.

Safety in the riding arena

As there are likely to be several horses and riders in a riding arena at any one time, it is necessary to observe certain safety precautions. Before you enter a school, whether it is indoor or out, knock on the door and call out 'Door free?' This lets the instructor or riders inside know that someone wishes to come in; imagine the chaos you could cause if you just flung open the door and marched in, straight into the path of a cantering horse!

Whoever is in the school will reply 'Door free' when it is safe for you to enter. Go into the school as quickly and quietly as possible, shutting the door behind you and all the time being aware of what is happening around you. The same procedure occurs if for some reason you need to leave the arena before everyone else.

Go into the middle of the school to mount up so that anyone working in the arena can continue to ride without you being in the way. If you need to stop during a lesson to alter stirrups etc, turn into the middle of the school.

Riding can be pretty hot work and there is bound to be a time when you need to remove your jacket. Turn into the middle of the school and ask your instructor if she will hold your horse while you take off your coat. This is because anything could happen to startle your horse and

there may be a nasty accident if someone is not on hand.
If there is no-one to help, dismount and remove your jacket.
Remember to keep your distance and do not use another
horse's bottom as a buffer and a way of stopping your horse. If you
are moving slower than other people move on to the inner track. Riders
moving at a faster pace have precedence so be aware of where
everyone else is.

As everyone may be going in different directions remember to pass
another rider left hand to left hand and to give each other plenty of
room. Do not ride across the approaches or landings of any jumps
which happen to be in the school if anyone is using them.

Working without stirrups

You will reach a point in your lessons when your instructor asks you
to 'quit and cross your stirrups' and you will find yourself working without
stirrups. This type of work will help you to develop a deeper seat as
well as improve your balance and feel for the horse. At first you should
only work for short periods without stirrups as it can be very tiring.
If you have not undertaken this type of exercise before and are asked
to do so by someone who is not familiar with your riding, you should
point this out.

All kinds of exercises and movements can be conducted without
stirrups: walking, trotting, cantering, jumping — there's a place for
sensible work minus your stirrups in all of these.

To cross your stirrups, pull the buckle end away from the stirrup bar.

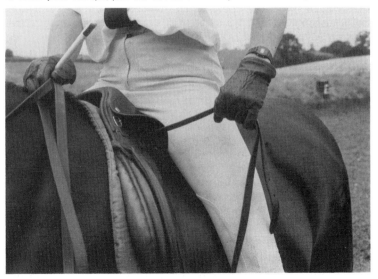

Above Then take hold of the stirrup iron and cross the stirrup over so that it lies on the horse's neck in front of the saddle.

Below For your own comfort ensure that the leathers lie as flat as possible under the saddle skirt. Cross the right stirrup over first.

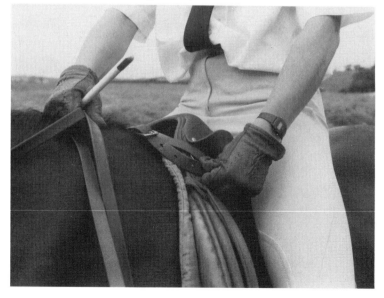

Above Working without stirrups is hard work at first, but persevere and you will reap the many benefits of this exercise.

Below Safety first when turning horses out into fields — always turn the horses to face the gate.

When you take your stirrups back, particularly after carrying out flat work exercises, your normal stirrup length will feel very short as your seat will have deepened and you may need to adjust your stirrups accordingly.

Turning out

If you are on one of the last rides of the day at your riding school you may be asked to help turn the horses out in the paddocks.

Check that all tack and boots have been removed and, in colder weather, find out if the horse needs a rug on before being turned out. Find out what the policy is in relation to head-collars, too; some owners always leave the horse with a head-collar on, others do just the opposite.

Give yourself plenty of room to go through the field gate and make sure that it does not swing back on you, the horse or anyone following. Close the gate before letting any horses loose. Once in the field you should turn the horse around so that he is facing the gate. You can then remove the head-collar and/or lead rope. If you just go through the gate and let the horse go you are in danger of being kicked if he suddenly takes advantage of his freedom.

RIDING OUT

There is a world of difference between riding in the confines of an indoor or outdoor school and taking to the road on a horse. Hacking out is part of every rider's education and most schools organize rides out for suitably competent clients. Such a ride will certainly add interest to your riding career and, if conducted properly, should increase your confidence.

Road sense

In some areas riding schools are not even remotely close to a road whereas others have to endure major roads on their doorstep. For your first excursion into the 'outside' world it is even more important for you to be mounted on a thoroughly reliable animal and accompanied by experienced riders.

Of course, it is not necessarily feasible to go out on a one instructor to one pupil basis, but rides should not be made up of tremendous numbers of riders, all of vastly differing abilities. There ought to be an instructor or an experienced person at the front and rear of the ride.

It is even more necessary when riding outside that you remain alert. You must be aware of your horse and the surroundings. While it is the responsibility of the person leading the hack to issue directions and signals for turning, to slow down traffic etc, there is no reason why you should not learn your Highway Code and all you can about riding on the roads.

Keep to the left hand side of the road. Although you can ride on grass verges, never ride across anyone's front garden or verge and do not ride on the footpath. Riders are often tempted to canter along grass verges but this is not a good idea, because there may be large holes which you cannot see until it is too late. Long grass could also hide dangerous rubbish such as broken glass, and anyway it is far safer to keep to walk and trot when riding on roads. If you were cantering along a verge and the horse shied you could easily be unseated, and, if you were heading for home, the horse may take hold and you could find yourself out of control.

Enjoying a safe hack.

You can ride in pairs, side by side, along the road with the younger or less-experienced rider/horse on the inside and away from the traffic. This way cars cannot squeeze past and so have to slow down to overtake you. However, the road must be wide enough for two horses ridden abreast plus a car; if the road is narrow ride in single file. If you cannot see whether there is any oncoming traffic, as you are approaching a bend or the brow of a hill for example, then ride in single file.

Always thank motorists who show you consideration. Not only is this good manners, but it also encourages drivers to slow down the next time they see a horse and rider. You can show consideration to others too, by giving cyclists and pedestrians plenty of room if you have to pass them.

In common with other road users you have to obey the rules of the road, so it is vital to know what all the signs and signals mean. You have to obey the police and traffic lights, just as the motorist does.

Your riding school hack should be organized so that the less-experienced riders are in the middle of the group and the leading file should keep a steady pace, tuned to the needs of the slowest member of the group. This way no-one will get left behind or have to struggle to keep up.

If you come to a road junction the whole party should cross the road together, rather than have the group split on either side of the road.

For your part, do not ride along with reins like washing lines — you

Before you move off, check behind.

need to be able to control your horse at all times. Have your whip, if you are carrying one, in your right hand. Notice what the instructor and the experienced rider at the rear of the ride are doing, then you will be able to learn about roadcraft for future rides out. For your guidance here is what should happen.

Before moving off, a rider should check behind to see what traffic is coming. A quick glance is not enough — the rider should be able to turn from the waist and look over her right shoulder so she has a good view of the road behind. A signal is required to show that the rider is intending to move off, so the arm is held out straight from the shoulder with the hand open and the palm facing forwards. Another check behind is needed before the rider takes hold of both reins again and moves off.

As you approach any road junction you need to check behind for traffic and put your reins and whip into the appropriate hand so that you can signal your intentions. If you are turning left you then need to halt behind the white line — whether it is a stop or give way line — and check for traffic by looking left, right and left again. When the road is clear look behind again, signal left, take hold of both reins again and make the turn.

When you are driving a car or riding a bicycle and you wish to turn right at a junction, you move into the centre of the road once you have checked the traffic and signalled. However, on a horse the procedure is different. You stay on the **left** side of the road. The checks before

*The rights and wrongs of riding on the road. Our rider on the left-hand side of the picture is demonstrating the correct position for negotiating a right turn, while her riding companion on the right shows how it definitely should **not** be done!*

and after halting at the white line are the same at any junction, but always make sure that your signals are very clear. As you cross the road keep looking up and down in case any traffic suddenly appears.

If you need to pass stationary cars or any other hazards such as road works, always check behind and ahead for traffic. It is sensible to wait rather than try passing a hazard at the same time as other traffic. Remember that dogs in parked cars may suddenly bark and upset your horse, so if you keep the horse's head slightly turned towards the traffic it will not be able to swing its back end into the path of the cars.

Hopefully the amount of road work you have to do from your riding school will be minimal and on quiet roads, but even when you are riding along bridleways there is a code of practice which is aimed at keeping everyone safe. Remember to keep your distance between horses just as you would in an manège. If you are riding virtually on top of each other, it will be dangerous if someone falls off.

If you do see someone fall off shout 'Loose horse' to let the person at the front of the ride know someone is off, and stop your own horse so that you can help the fallen rider. You may hear a yell behind you, so look round as it is quite possible someone has fallen off and needs help.

Safety and country sense

Some schools make good use of hacks to increase their
pupils' skill and confidence; along a bridleway for example you
may be asked one by one to trot on and away from the group to a
certain point, halt and wait for the rest of the ride. You may also be
split into smaller groups for a canter. You will be able to ride away from
the group at a faster pace than when you ride towards them. Don't
forget that it is a natural instinct for horses to be with their friends so
they are going to be keener to return to the group. You must be careful
that this keenness does not get out of hand, otherwise the horse will
simply rush back to his friends.

Unless you can control a horse reasonably well you ought not to
be allowed on hacks. However, you will probably find that the horses
are more onward-bound outside, and even the most docile ones have
a little more sparkle about them when cantering in the open.

The horses will no doubt know the routes of hacks around their home
area better than you, so you may find some of them anticipating the
next stage of the hack. If they always canter along a certain stretch
they will be ready to go before you even know it is a cantering place,
and they probably know exactly where the slowing point is too.

Listen carefully to the directions from your instructor and then try
to stick to them. Don't go flying past the whole ride unless you really
cannot help it. But what should you do if you lose control?

People often think the horse has bolted with them when in fact it
hasn't. You may experience a horse becoming rather strong and pulling
on, but this is completely different to a horse which is bolting. In the
latter case the horse seems to be in a blind panic and does not take
any notice of where it is going.

If the horse does start to get rather strong what can you do? Firstly,
try not to panic and don't start yelling or screaming. It is highly likely
that the horse will stop anyway as soon as he comes to the usual
stopping place: you need to make sure you are still with him.

Yelling will only upset the horse further and does not help the
situation at all. Make a bridge of your reins across the horse's neck
so that he is pulling against himself and it is not so easy for him to
pull you forward off balance. Take hold of the mane or martingale neckstrap for extra security if you wish.

Make sure that you sit up and brace your feet firmly in the stirrups.
There is no point in just hauling continuously on both reins as you are
just giving the horse something to pull against. You can pull, relax, pull,
relax and so on to try and slow the horse down. This way he cannot
set his jaw and neck muscles against you.

If you are stable enough in the saddle to be able to attempt to stop
the horse you can anchor one hand on his neck and give a series of
short, sharp pulls on the other rein. This can unbalance the horse so

it is not advisable on a very slippery surface.

Another method for slowing down involves turning the horse in a large circle but obviously a great deal of room is needed for this. Whatever you do, try not to tip forward, because when the horse does stop you will go straight over his head. Remember too that horses can swerve quite quickly, so don't expect the horse to stop in a straight line as soon as he's caught up with his friends or reached the usual stopping place. Sit down in the saddle and sit tall.

Riding around the countryside may also involve going across some undulating terrain, steep banks and hills. For the horse to balance himself across rough ground, up and down hills, he needs freedom of his head and neck so the rider must allow him this. The rider's balance and seat needs to be good enough without having to resort to hanging on to the horse's head.

When riding up a steep hill the rider needs to be well forward, with his weight over his knees so that the horse's back is freed of the rider's weight. Have the reins relatively slack and take hold of the horse's mane about halfway up his neck. Alternatively, take hold of the martingale strap. On no account pull backwards on the reins as you could easily upset the horse's balance.

If you have to come down a steep slope, ride straight down. Do not start zigzagging your way down as if the horse slips with one foot he will fall. Give the horse the freedom of his head and neck but be ready to steer him round an obstacle. Do not tip forward or lean too far back as that is only making life more awkward for the horse. Long-distance riders, who frequently ride across all types of territory, tend to sit tall in the saddle, taking their weight down through their legs.

If you ride through woodland or across flinty or stony ground let the horse choose his route, but keep your eyes open so that if he needs to be guided away from a hazard you can help.

Remember that the horse has been on this ride many more times than you have and will be able to cope. The horse needs a rider who is not going to be a cumbersome and interfering passenger. If you feel at all insecure hold the mane and have faith in your horse. No horse will fall down or get himself into trouble if he can possibly avoid it.

If you have to cross streams or rivers stay calm and remember that the horses will have taken many riders across on previous hacks. Give the horse enough rein so he can balance himself, particularly if the bank is rather steep and hold on to the mane if you feel apprehensive about descending into the water. Keep a firm seat in the saddle.

When you are in the water be ready to kick your feet free of the stirrups if your horse should stumble. Otherwise, stay as still as you can in order to help the horse recover his footing. If you are standing still in a stream be aware that some horses will roll; a foreleg thrashing in the water is sometimes a sign that the animal is about to go down and roll. If you are worried that your mount may be considering this, keep his head up and get him on the move.

Some areas of the country have some superb riding country which is reached via narrow, slippery country roads. The feeling of being on a horse which is slipping on a road is rather unnerving, especially for novice riders. Give the horse plenty of rein and hold on to the mane. If the road is particularly bad or steep then your instructor may ask you all to dismount and lead the horses for part of the way. Do not forget to run up the stirrups or cross them over the saddle and lead with the horse's reins over his head, unless he is wearing a martingale.

Gates are another feature of the countryside which add interest to a hack out. On your first rides it is likely that someone else will open and close all the gates for you, but it is useful, especially if you decide to have your own horse, to learn the knack of negotiating gates. You may find you develop your own way to suit your own horse, but here is one method.

To open a gate you need to position your horse parallel to the gate, with his head facing the latch. You can then take your reins and whip in one hand and undo the latch with the hand nearest the gate. If you then use your leg nearest the gate to ask the horse to move sideways through a hundred degrees you should be able to pull open the gate and push it aside. Your horse's head will be facing the gate but it is important that you do not catch him (or anyone else) with the gate and do not let him stretch his head forward to scratch himself on the gate as part of his bridle may get caught up in the latch.

You can then pass through the gate, taking care that it does not swing back on to you or any following riders. Then you need to turn round, close the gate and fasten the latch, keeping the horse parallel to the gate again.

Some horses are well-behaved at gates and will stand parallel to the gate while you undo the latch and then move sideways at the same time as the rider is opening the gate. Others do not like gates and try to rush through, so be careful that they do not knock your knees and legs on the gateposts as they go through the gate.

It is quite possible that another new experience on some of your later hacks out will be galloping — although this may not be intentional! Gallop is an extension of the canter, and if you wish to gallop you ask your horse to canter and once this is established you use both legs to urge the horse forwards into gallop.

The three-time pace of the canter changes into a four-time pace for the gallop, the sequence being:

1. Near-hind
2. Off-hind
3. Near-fore
4. Off-fore

A useful skill to acquire is that of opening and closing gates without having to dismount.

There is also a period of suspension before the next cycle of four-time movement begins.

This is a very comfortable pace for the rider particularly if you adopt a lighter seat by standing on the stirrups with your seat just out of the saddle, body inclining forwards slightly, knees and ankles acting as shock absorbers. You will find it easier to go with the horse and you are helping him too.

Finally, whenever you ride out observe the country code as well as the Highway Code. Only ride over fields if there is a bridleway (and you should keep to the designated route although if this goes across crops it makes more sense to ride around the edge of the field) or if you have permission from the owner. Public footpaths are not intended for horse riders.

Always leave gates as you found them and if you are using a bridleway which passes through fields of grazing animals be very careful when opening and closing gates. It is probably easier to dismount so you can ensure that none of the livestock slips through the gate and makes a bid for freedom.

Ride sensibly through fields where there is livestock, especially at certain times of the year, eg when sheep are lambing. If you gallop through a field of ewes at this time you could easily terrify them, leading to miscarriages. Treat other people's land and property with respect, just as you would wish yours to be treated.

Do not ride through crops. Be courteous to other countryside users. Come back to a walk to pass people as not everyone is familiar with horses; some people are simply frightened by the sheer size of a horse.

Stay alert and your hacks in the countryside can be so much safer and enjoyable.

LEARNING TO JUMP

Everyone wants to learn to jump, the problem being that most riders are anxious to take this step before they are actually ready. Learning to jump is great fun but first you need to have a firm, independent seat and to be able to stay in balance with the horse on the flat. Having mastered this you can go on to improve your riding by learning to jump, for in addition to helping your balance and control, jumping will improve your co-ordination of aids, sharpen up your reactions and give you increased feel and awareness of the horse's movements.

As you progress to gymnastic jumping exercises and riding courses you will find that your brain is put to the test again. Even a series of small fences can be quite a challenge, requiring considerable thought and positive riding.

There are differing views on whether horses are natural jumpers. It is certainly true that some horses have a natural talent for it and enjoy using their skill. Others, however, are extremely difficult when it comes to expending energy over jumps. In the wild a horse would jump an obstacle in its way if it was fleeing from an enemy and, as owners of escapist horses and ponies know, some animals are adept at leaping out of their fields to go 'walkabout' or to join friends in a neighbouring field.

When a horse leaps over an obstacle he is lengthening and elevating his stride. Different types of obstacles and different heights affect the amount of lengthening and elevation. For instance, over a cavaletti (a small jump measuring about 45cm (18in) high) there would be a little elevation of the stride but lengthening is unlikely, whereas if a steeplechase fence was tackled, there would be considerable elevation and lengthening.

Position

As with any movement in riding it is essential that the rider stays in balance with the horse. As the horse jumps he stretches his head and neck so his centre of gravity moves forward. To stay in balance the rider therefore has to move forward so over a fence the rider adopts the jumping position; that is she should:

1. Fold from the hips — the size of the fence will dictate how much the rider needs to fold
2. Maintain a straight back
3. Look ahead
4. Follow the movement of the horse's head with her hands — as the horse jumps he stretches his neck so the rider must keep a light contact and allow for this movement. This is where supple, tension-free arms and shoulders are necessary to ensure a sympathetic 'following' of the horse.
5. Maintain leg position
6. Keep light contact of seat with saddle or, over bigger fences, seat a little out of the saddle

Before you actually jump a fence your instructor will have you practising this lighter seat, at halt, walk, trot and canter to help you find your balance.

For jumping shorten your stirrups at least two holes from your normal flatwork length. This closes the angles at your knees, hips and ankles so it should be easier for you to balance your upper body. Folding from the hips is much easier and more comfortable with shorter stirrups than it is with longer ones. Why not try both positions and see for yourself?

As you fold, you should be able to feel your weight go down via your knees to the balls of your feet. Do not let your legs slip backwards. They should remain in the usual position, in contact with the horse's sides. If you do not maintain your leg position, you will not be able to apply any effective aids.

In addition to supporting your weight, your knees and ankles act as shock absorbers when you land after a jump and this is one of the reasons why they need to be supple. Excess tension anywhere in your body affects your ability to absorb the horse's movement and so you could find your body being rather jarred every time you land after a fence.

Try not to grip with your knees too much. Concentrate on your bent knee and on the weight going down through your lower leg, rather than clamping your knees on to the saddle and your lower legs into the horse's sides.

All the exercises to open up and increase the suppleness of your hips will be appreciated once you start jumping. For it is your ability to open and close the angle of your hips (ie your aptitude for folding your body) which will help you to keep in harmony with the horse.

Introduction to jumping

Your first rung on the jumping ladder will be poles placed on the ground over which you may walk or trot. It is also a useful exercise to canter over poles on the ground but this is generally used for more experienced riders.

Depending on the pace and the stride of the horse or pony concerned, the distance between the poles varies. What you need to concentrate on is keeping the horse going forwards in a good rhythm.

Your equine partner for these first lessons ought to be an obliging character who will not rush at the poles, stop or dive out at the last minute. All animals have their off-days but if your school cannot provide you with a suitable mount for learning to jump then you may be better to look elsewhere for instruction. You do not want these early lessons to turn into a fight with a stroppy animal or to become a frightening experience for you.

Some schools take the sensible precaution of providing neckstraps so if you feel unsure of yourself you can take hold of the strap for extra security. There is nothing cowardly in this; it is simply helping you and protecting the horse from an unnecessary jab in the mouth. If neckstraps are not provided then hold on to the horse's mane.

With trotting poles you will build up so that you are trotting down a line of poles while maintaining rising trot. Look where you are going, not at the ground, and think of the horse keeping a good, regular rhythm as he trots down the line of poles. You may feel the horse stretch his neck and lower his head over the poles so be ready to give with your hands and let him stretch.

Aim for the centre of the poles unless told otherwise. Sometimes, if there are both ponies and horses in a lesson, the trotting poles will be fanned out so that at one end the distance is right for the ponies while at the other end they are further apart and suitable for the longer striding horses.

Give yourself plenty of room as you approach and leave the line of poles. If you try any tight turns you will probably lose your rhythm and it will be difficult to straighten up in time.

The next step is for the instructor to add a small jump a little way beyond the last trotting pole. Usually crossed poles are used as the cross helps to guide the horse and novice riders to the centre of the fence. The procedure is to trot down the line of poles as before and pop over the little jump. Just because there is a small obstacle in the way do not become over-anxious and start throwing yourself forward in an elaborate impression of a top show-jumper tackling the big wall in puissance competitions!

You are hardly likely to feel a tremendous difference between the sensation of going over the poles and this small jump. The horse certainly does not have to make a tremendous effort and as you should be in harmony with him, there is no need for you to make terrific efforts either.

You may be asked by your instructor to let the horse have a loose rein for this exercise just in case you do get left behind the movement. If you do find yourself taking the jump out of balance with the horse and behind the movement (it will seem as if you are trying to catch up with the horse) then slip your reins, ie open your fingers so that the reins slip through and you do not jerk the horse in the mouth.

Remember to look ahead and wait for the jump to come to you. There is a good reason for not anticipating too much — imagine where you would land if you adopted an exaggerated jumping position way before you needed to and the horse suddenly tripped over! Be ready to fold your body forwards so you go with the horse. 'With' is the important word; you should be aiming to be **with** the horse, not jumping the fence **before** or **after** him.

It may take some time for you to accustom yourself to the feeling of a horse jumping and to 'tune in' to the process, especially as it is very easy to throw a horse off balance if you suddenly fall forward during the last few strides, for example, or throw the reins away just before the horse takes off.

Methods of teaching jumping vary considerably but the emphasis should be on safety and building confidence by taking gradual steps, ensuring that the rider is quite happy about everything mastered so far and is keen to continue. If you do find that the lessons are proving too difficult or if you are frightened, then go back to the beginning. You are riding for fun so do not let anyone make your riding lesson miserable.

Some instructors will have you jumping single fences, both uprights and spreads, after your introduction to jumping via trotting poles. Others will make use of small fences and placing poles in a line or grid before moving on to jumping single fences. Whatever method of instruction you come across, always try to ride your horse forwards positively and concentrate on establishing your balance in harmony with the horse.

An important point that beginners often forget is to keep their legs on the horse. This helps to keep the horse in a good rhythm as he approaches and leaves the fence, helps him to jump the obstacle and keeps the rhythm going in between fences.

The horse's hindquarters have already been described as his engine. If you work a horse by using your legs to encourage his hind legs to come further underneath his body, then he will be better able to tackle an obstacle. As his hind legs come through under his body, so the horse's forehand lightens, making it easier for him to come off the ground. On the other hand, if you stop using your legs and let the horse drag his hindlegs, his whole body will become longer, more weight will go on to his forehand and it will be more difficult for the horse to jump well.

Of course, keeping a good rhythm and balance all the time takes a great deal of effort and practice. With some riding school horses it will be very hard work, but even so it makes sense to know what you are after and try to achieve it.

You will find that working through grids teaches you to keep your legs on the horse and later, when you are riding competitively or have your own animal, you will discover that sometimes you get into trouble and then it is vital to keep your legs on to help the horse. Gridwork also helps to establish your position, increase your suppleness, speed up your reactions and build your confidence.

If the horse is jumping well it is easier for the rider to jump well too, but first the rider has to understand what happens to the horse when jumping and the horse needs to know what is required of him.

In the approach to a jump the horse will weigh up the obstacle, stretching and lowering his head and neck so he can judge his take off point. In order to take off, the horse raises his head and shortens his neck to help bring his forehand off the ground while his hind legs come in well under his body to provide the propulsive power. The horse stretches his head and neck in the flight over the jump, his forelegs are tucked up and he should be jumping with a rounded back. His hindlegs are tucked up underneath his belly and as his forelegs extend ready for landing so the horse's head and neck come up again. This enables him to land with as little shock and concussion as possible. As the hindlegs come down so he can get into his stride and continue on his way.

Until you are jumping the larger fences you do not really feel the horse descending from the jump. However, irrespective of the size of the jump, the horse needs as much help as possible from the rider and as little interference as possible. That can only be achieved by good instruction and plenty of practice.

JUMPING AND RIDING COURSES

After your early lessons on learning to jump fences there are a wide range of exercises you can do to improve your balance, confidence, agility and timing.

Improving your technique

Working through grids of five or six jumps in line is particularly useful. You can work in either trot or canter although from the point of view of both horse and rider canter is much easier. In trot a horse has to use himself more while this pace also requires a better sense of timing from the rider. It is far easier to stay with a horse's movement over the fence when you approach in canter.

Your exercises through the grid may include knotting your reins and dropping them on to the horse's neck as you go over the fences, picking them up again as you land over the last jump. From this you can progress to riding down the line with your arms folded, stretched out to the sides or behind. You will soon find that you really do not need the reins for balance.

Once you have established a safe secure seat work without stirrups can be included. Gymnastic jumping (ie using grids) is a superb way of building up your confidence and suppleness. You also soon learn how to use your legs to keep the horse going fluently through the exercise.

A golden rule of jumping is never to try to do too much or to frighten yourself; it can take only seconds to lose confidence but months to restore it. To some extent your instructor has to push you along, but if you really are worried about any fence, say so. It is far better to continue going over smaller jumps until you are anxious to move up than to be bullied into tackling larger fences when you are not ready.

If you are quite happy about jumping then more treats are in store as you progress to jumping small courses, and hopefully, if your riding school has the facilities, to jumping cross-country fences.

The big difference between show-jumping and cross-country jumping is that the jumps in the latter do not fall down if you hit them!

Show-jumps are coloured, artificial fences and the course is contained in a relatively small area; cross-country jumps make use of natural obstacles such as hedges, ditches and banks. Although a cross-country course is specifically built for the purpose just as a show-jumping course is, the fences use rustic rather than coloured poles. A cross-country course usually covers quite a large area, too — about a mile and a quarter would be a typical length, compared to around three or four hundred metres for a show-jumping course. Whichever type of course you are riding, you need to keep the horse going forwards in a good, active rhythm and to give him every chance to jump the fences well. Avoid sharp turns into fences or the poor horse barely has time to see the fence, never mind jump it!

Let us look at the type of fences you can meet, both in show-jumping and in cross-country riding.

Novice-level show-jumping

As far as show-jumps are concerned, there are basically two types, the upright and the spread, yet within these types there is a whole host of variations; uprights can be presented in the form of walls, planks, poles and gates, while spreads can include triple bars, parallels, water and a hog's back. There is even a fence which is a cross between an upright and a spread fence — the fan jump.

The fences can be presented in various combinations to really test the ability of horse and rider, eg as a double or treble with two and three elements to the fence respectively. How the jumps are placed in relation to each other and to other factors such as the collecting ring or entrance to the arena also has a bearing. For instance, a fence on the diagonal going away from the collecting ring often catches people out; their horses are not so keen to go on away from other equine friends and a refusal or a knock down often results.

So when riding a course there is quite a lot to think about — and that is before you come to the exciting aspects like riding against the clock. It really is a case of learning by doing when it comes to riding courses. If you have had a good grounding in gymnastic jumping then you will be better prepared for courses. After all, your reactions will be quicker and you will be able to recover quickly from a jump and be ready to ride for the next fence.

Keep in your mind the thought of maintaining the rhythm. One easy way of doing this is to think about cantering around the arena in a good, balanced, rhythmic canter. Do not think about the jumps; they just happen to be in the way. It is amazing how this does help.

Remember to aim for the centre of each jump, look ahead and use your legs. Do not worry about not being able to see a stride so you can tell the horse when to take off. Your horse should be far more experienced than you so he ought to be able to make his own judgements. Just keep him going forwards strongly and be ready to go with him.

By this stage you should be able to maintain a good contact on the reins, but do not throw it away at the last moment. You should have a definite but allowing contact. The horse will be used to the rider having a contact over the jump and will feel rather insecure if he is suddenly let down by the rider dropping the contact.

The only time you should drop the contact (also known as slipping the reins) is if you realize you are in trouble and you should then allow the horse absolute freedom of his head and neck so that he can help himself as best as possible. However, you should be ready to pick up the horse again, ie resume a contact and ride on after you have landed.

Never look down at the bottom of a fence or that is where you will land. When riding through combinations look ahead through the whole sequence and ride every element — don't collapse in delight after successfully negotiating the first part!

If you make a mistake at one fence on the course, forget it and ride on positively. There is no point in looking back at a pole on the ground when you have another few fences in front of you. Once you have completed your round you can look back over the whole course with your instructor and analyze where improvements could have been made.

Riding small courses well and then discovering how you can take less time by riding smooth turns is a satisfying experience. Go out and try it — and if your riding school cannot provide you with good instruction, try a holiday course. There are centres where you can get tuition from people who have been successful competitors in the show-jumping world.

Cross-country riding

One of the most exciting aspects of riding is jumping across country. There is so much variety and challenge that even the smallest of courses can give you a tremendous sense of achievement. Most schools have a few cross-country fences, while the larger centres often have complete courses. Fences can be a combination of ordinary uprights and spreads; fences which have no height but which produce their own problems, eg ditches and water; drops; banks; and fences either situated into, out of or in the middle of water.

It is very important that any cross-country course is well-built from sturdy materials, as horses respect solid fences and will generally jump them well. Often a cross-country course is more off-putting to the rider than the horse.

Upright fences, whether cross-country or show-jumps, are approached in the same way, and as the horse finds this type of fence most difficult to judge you must not ride in too fast. Combination fences need the same type of consideration so that the horse has time to see what is expected of him.

Try to achieve a nice round bouncy canter, so that you feel as if the horse has a lot of power which you can unleash simply by asking. If you let the horse get into a long drawn out shape it will be much more difficult for him to jump anything.

Spread fences need a little more speed whilst still holding the horse together, so that the horse can jump well out (as opposed to simply going 'up and down') in order to clear the furthest part of the jump. One of the most difficult jumps is a true parallel as the horse cannot see the furthest bar very well, so it is up to the rider to approach very strongly on an increasing, rather than a decreasing, stride. You will be glad of any gridwork you have done here as it really teaches you to use your legs strongly.

Ditches and drop fences also need strong, positive riding. A horse may not see a ditch until very late and anyway a hole in the ground is hardly inviting! You need to let the horse see the ditch but do not emphasize it too much. If you dally too long the horse may get his head down, start backing off the obstacle and eventually grind to a halt, so you need to look ahead and ride forwards strongly. Drop fences feel much better if the horse is ridden on strongly so that he lands further out, rather than hopping over the fence and dropping down too vertically.

Jumps into and out of water need strong riding, holding the horse together with the legs ready to give him very strong aids if he suddenly falters. Beware of jumping too fast into water as if it is deep there is quite a drag from the water when you land.

If you want to see how cross-country fences should be ridden, watch some of the top event riders like Lucinda Green and Virginia Leng in action, either by attending horse trials in person or watching the television coverage of Badminton and Burghley three-day events. Training videos are also available which are ideal for examining a rider's style.

When you get to this stage you will realize how important all the flatwork and attaining of an independent seat has been. Balance is extremely important and so is co-ordination of your aids. It is for experiences like the thrill of riding across country that you should have spent time early on in your riding career gaining a sound foundation.

Jumping is fun and with practice it becomes much easier, yet you will still come across problems, such as horses refusing or running out. Do not look upon these difficulties as real setbacks, but use them as an opportunity to learn more, to acquire confidence in dealing with situations which are not always going to plan, to think solutions through yourself. You will have greater understanding and awareness of the horse and rider partnership as a result.

A horse may stop at a fence for several reasons:

1. Association of jumping with pain because he was jabbed in the mouth by a heavy-handed, off balance rider.

2. Association with pain because of injury such as a sore back or legs, or ill-fitting tack.

3. Bad presentation of the horse to the fence by the rider.

4. The horse sensing that the rider's heart really is not in it.

5. The rider not telling the horse what to do — sometimes riders do freeze and no longer give any aids. The horse therefore wonders what he is supposed to do.

6. An inexperienced horse finds himself at a bad distance from the fence and may stop because he does not yet have the confidence or skill to know how to jump himself out of trouble.

7. The horse is just too lazy and did not receive positive enough aids.

If the horse you are riding stops at a fence establish the reason and then you can attempt the fence again, providing you have tried to solve the problem and brought the horse in on a better line of approach, more actively or whatever.

A horse which runs out usually does so because of an error on the rider's part, such as trying to jump the fence from too sharp an angle, or going at the jump too fast (it is always more difficult to control your direction if the horse is too onward bound).

Siting of the jump can cause problems, too. Watch at any show and you will see the animals who try to rush back to the collecting ring rather than jump the fence which the course builder has placed near the entrance. It is up to the rider to bring the horse in to the jump in a much more controlled and determined fashion. If the horse has run out to the right then next time approach from the right with your whip carried in the right hand too. Slow down, approach the fence in trot and then ride on strongly once you are set up for the fence. Think of the tunnel provided by your legs and hands in which the horse should move; keep looking straight ahead and be determined.

Some riders are said to have 'electric bottoms' because they always seem to fire up horses. Quite often this is because the rider is nervous, becomes tense and this is transmitted to the horse. The result can be that the horse rushes his fences. Other reasons for horses approaching a jump too fast include the animal being afraid or in pain; he rushes in order to get the ordeal over as quickly as possible.

If the problem stems from the rider then lessons on the flat, either on the lunge or in a class, should be substituted for the jumping lessons to build up confidence. Horses who have bad memories of jumping require considerable time and patience to restore their confidence.

Always be ready to learn and bear in mind that horses are great levellers so although something may be really difficult today, tomorrow you could be flying high. Keep an open mind and never think that you cannot or do not need to improve. That way riding will always be an enjoyable challenge.

WHAT NEXT?

After a few months of riding lessons there are bound to be a few questions bouncing around in your mind. Am I progressing fast enough? Would I be all right on a riding holiday? Would I be able to find a horse to take to a small competition? Could I cope with my own horse? How can I find out?

It is natural that once you have mastered the basics of anything you start to look for new challenges. This book has given you an introduction to the pleasures of riding, but if you wish to delve further into the delights of this sport there is a whole host of routes open to you.

Examinations

These are not as bad as they sound! The Association of British Riding Schools has a series of ten tests designed specifically for the weekly rider. They are open to anyone over nine years of age who rides regularly at an ABRS school.

Each level involves a combination of riding and stable managment, ie horse-care, so if you aspire to be a horse owner these tests are a particularly valuable monitor of your knowledge. You must take the tests in order and although the first stage is fairly basic the standards are generally very high. The tests are comprehensive and you need a good knowledge of your subject.

There's a minimal charge for each test and apart from the satisfaction of passing you receive a certificate and a coloured felt to be worn under the ABRS badge.

The British Horse Society also runs a series of examinations. In an attempt to educate riders about roadcraft they devised the Riding and Road Safety Test which is open to anyone between the ages of 10 and 65. If you have to ride on the roads it is sensible to know as much as possible about the Highway Code, how it relates to horses and how you should conduct yourself on the road. You can find out more about the Riding and Road Safety Test by contacting your local BHS representative or BHS headquarters at Stoneleigh. They, or your local riding club, will be able to tell you when the next test is being held.

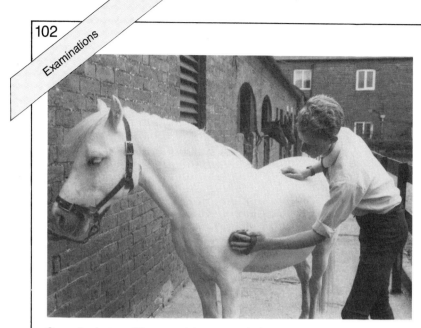

Grooming is one of the many jobs you can help with, either at your local riding school or assisting a private owner, and it is all good practice in case you decide to have a go at horsey exams.

You will need access to a horse.

Before the actual test you will attend a practical demonstration, a lecture and undergo some training. On the day itself you will be asked questions on the Highway Code and there will be a tack and turnout safety inspection. You then ride along a simulated road route to see how you cope with the hazards, give road signals and cope in traffic before you are sent out for a proper road test.

There is a certificate for the successful candidates plus the knowledge that they are doing all they can to make themselves safe on the roads. The BHS produces an excellent booklet on roadcraft which is available from them for a small fee. A small charge is also made for the test itself. It is always worth asking if your riding school would be prepared to run a test day and let their clients take the exam on school horses.

The British Horse Society also has a series of Horse Knowledge and Riding Stages examinations. These are graded and are especially useful if you wish to pursue a career with horses. For instance, to become a BHS Assistant Instructor you need to have passed Stages I, II and III, as well as the Riding and Road Safety Test plus the Preliminary Teaching Test.

The Horse Knowledge and Riding Stages have recently been revised and upgraded so they present quite a challenge to all riders, whether

horse owners or not. You can train towards these examinations at most BHS riding schools — ask the owner if there
are any other clients interested in forming a group to work
towards their Stages exams. As the testing is done at various
examination centres throughout the country there is a wide choice
of venues and dates. You do not need your own horse either, as you
ride the animals at the test centre.

These examinations are considerably more expensive than the
ABRS tests but of course they are also steps along the professional
ladder for those with horsey careers in mind. For details of costs, dates
and the syllabuses, contact the British Horse Society.

Luckily there is also something between the weekly rider tests and
the more demanding professional qualifications. Your local riding club
will run tests, again graded and involving both riding and stable
management. Standards are high as these are a type of non-
professional version of the BHS Stages. To be eligible you need to be
a member of a BHS affiliated riding club and tests are run according
to demand. You will need access to a horse for these but it is worth
asking if your riding school would let you hire one.

For the under-21s the Pony Club holds instructional rallies and runs
tests when necessary.

Some riding schools run their own proficiency tests and the
equestrian magazine *Horse & Pony* runs a Progress Scheme where
rosettes and certificates can be gained by those successful in riding
and horse-care tests. There is a series of ten progressive stages and
a nominal charge is made.

Holidays

You can combine instruction with a great deal of fun on a riding holiday
and there is certainly a wide choice available at centres all over Britain.

Some establishments provide an all-round instructional holiday
covering jumping, hacking out, stable management and schooling with
mini tests or competitions at the end of the week. Other centres
specialize in crash courses to prepare you for BHS exams, whilst others
offer intensive courses on particular aspects such as show-jumping,
eventing or dressage. You can holiday at centres where they will
introduce you to long-distance riding, driving or Western riding. If you
are aiming to become a horse owner there are plenty of centres where
you can own a horse for the week, so discovering the joys and
drawbacks of being totally responsible for an animal's welfare.

To some riders the attraction of a holiday lies in the chance to ride
in totally different country. There is a world of difference between riding
in an indoor school and cantering across the wide open spaces of
Exmoor. A week's holiday at a good centre can give you a tremendous
confidence boost.

Unfortunately, just as there are 'cowboy' riding schools, so there are some dubious holiday centres. If it is at all possible, visit the establishment before booking a holiday otherwise you could be very disappointed. Quite often one part of the holiday package is superb but another section of it leaves something to be desired.

Investigate the accommodation as it can be rather basic; find out whether it is caravans, shared rooms, bunk-beds, local guest-houses or some other form. Do ensure that the animals are in decent condition, that basic safety rules are followed and that instruction, if any is offered, is from suitable people.

Chat with your usual instructor before booking a holiday so you choose the best holiday for your capabilities. There is no point opting for pony trekking if you are a fairly competent rider looking to improve your skills. If the brochure says the holiday is for experienced or competent riders only, ring the centre owner and ask them precisely what they mean. 'Experienced' can cover anything from 'able to walk, trot and canter in control' to 'able to ride for 25 miles per day at speed on a fit Thoroughbred'.

If you are able to cope with long fast rides over open country, you will enjoy a trail riding holiday. These can vary from 20 to 30 miles per day over different areas but returning to the same base each night to a week's riding with stops at different accommodation each night.

A riding holiday need not necessarily exclude the non-riding members of your family either, as more and more centres are becoming flexible in their arrangements. Camping and self-catering holidays are also available at some centres, so the riders can have a great time while the whole family has an inexpensive holiday.

One point you will notice is that some areas offer remarkably cheap riding, but this is not necessarily a reflection on their standards. It is simply that in some regions it is cheaper than others to pursue this particular pastime.

You will see advertisements for equestrian holidays in the horsey press and many magazines also carry editorial reviews of centres. Be discerning here and take notice of the magazines whose staff have actually tried and tested the holidays.

Riding clubs

Throughout Britain there are riding clubs organizing all kinds of social, competitive and instructional activities. People often feel that there is no point in belonging to a club unless they have a horse yet there is **every** reason to join, since you can meet other horsey folk, lend a hand at the club shows and learn a great deal. You will see how courses are built, how various riders overcome problems and even discover which mistakes to avoid making in the show ring. Through regular

contact with horse owners you may well find someone who
needs help with their horse, even if it is only as a holiday relief.

There is the chance to take the riding club tests, if the club is
affiliated to the British Horse Society, and if you can hire a horse
you can take advantage of the courses which many clubs organize
with local personalities of the horse world. More and more top riders
are giving clinics in the winter months and these are often organized
in association with local riding clubs. These give you the chance to
learn a great deal for just a small outlay.

If you cannot compete on a horse there is always the inter-club quiz
evenings to demonstrate your knowledge. Talks with question and
answer sessions by vets, feed experts, farriers, the local huntsman
— all these social activities organized by your riding club will equip
you with a better understanding of the horse and the horse world. The
BHS will be able to tell you the secretary of your nearest riding club.

A few enterprising riding schools also have clubs for their clients,
organizing events in a similar way to the riding clubs. They usually
include competitions when the riding school horses are hired for small
amounts so that everyone has the chance of riding for rosettes. Apart
from being great fun to take part in, such events do stimulate interest
and loyalty in the riding school. If your school does not have a club,
why not start one?

Hiring horses for competitions

Your riding school may not advertise the fact, but it is quite possible
that the owner would let you hire a horse to take to a show. Of course
no-one's going to trust you if you have always acted irresponsibly with
horses, but provided you are competent and sensible, you will have
a good chance of finding someone who will oblige.

Later on, if your riding is good enough, you could aim at hiring a
hunter. Depending on your locality, this can be quite an easy task.
Whenever you borrow a horse, make sure you and the horse's owner
are quite clear about where responsibility lies if there is an accident
and the horse injures itself, you, another person or someone else's
property.

If you are unlucky enough to live in an area where you cannot hire
a horse for competitive or hunting purposes, there are mini-breaks
available at various holiday centres where you can take a horse to a
local show or go hunting.

Exercising other people's horses

One of the biggest problems for adult horse owners who are employed
full-time, is finding the spare hours to exercise a horse every day. Going
away on holiday can also be a headache as arrangements have to

be made to ensure that the horse is well cared for in the owner's absence.

It is worth placing an advertisement in the local saddlery shop or putting the word around your riding club, offering your services. You will probably have to undertake some stable tasks in exchange for rides, but it is all good experience.

Once you have found someone who needs help it is necessary to sort out the arrangements. You will need to discuss the times you will be able to ride, whether you are expected to make any kind of financial contribution, what the position would be if either you or the horse were injured whilst on a ride, whether the horse has any problems you should know about such as traffic, fear of pigs etc, whether there are any physical problems relating to the horse which need to be considered when riding out and so on.

Do not wait for a problem to arise before tackling it — any owner worth his salt will be only too keen to ensure that his horse receives the best possible care. Forethought and open discussion between the owner and rider can only be to everyone's advantage.

Even if you are only able to help someone as a holiday relief you will find the experience of riding privately-owned horses extremely valuable, but be careful when looking for a horse to ride, that you do not over-sell yourself. There is no point in pretending to yourself or anyone else that you are very experienced, used to problem horses, quite able to cope with fit hunters and so on. Horses are known to be great levellers so tell the truth — or the horse may literally 'drop you in it'!

Having a horse on loan

This is quite useful as a testing ground to discover whether you really do have the necessary commitment, time and money to cope with a horse. You will see advertisements in your local newspaper or saddlers for horses on loan or you may hear of one through a riding club. It is also possible to have a horse on loan from one of the recognized horse charities. Most charities will not sell their animals, but to relieve the pressure on their resources they will loan horses to suitable homes.

When a request for a loan is considered, a representative of the charity will visit you to inspect the place where you intend to keep the horse. If they are satisfied that you have sufficient knowledge and resources to give a horse a caring, loving home they will arrange a loan as soon as a suitable animal becomes available. There is a small fee for this service and although the horse is still the property of the charity, its everyday welfare is your responsibility.

Unless your circumstances change and you can no longer afford the horse, or the charity feels that you are not giving the horse a good home, the horse is with you on permanent loan. Inspections by the charity are arranged at regular intervals to ensure that the animal's best interests are catered for at all times.

The only obstacle in loaning from a charity is that the number of riding horses can be limited so you may have to wait a while. In addition, the animals for loan may have particular problems relating to their past, such as being difficult to handle in the stable because of ill treatment by a previous owner. However, if you can give a charity horse a home, you will benefit and you will also be generally helping the cause of horse welfare.

Charities apart, there are a number of animals available each year for loan. Often their owners cannot bear to part with their first and now outgrown animals which have given them so much fun. Horses whose owners are away at college or belonging to people with young families also need temporary homes.

If you wish to have an animal on loan ask all your local contacts, riding club secretaries, saddlers and farriers. Remember though, that you will be responsible for the animal's keep so it is worth compiling a budget to see whether you can actually afford to loan a horse or not.

Some owners insist that you keep the horse at a certain establishment, but more often than not you will have to find suitable accommodation for the horse. It is also your task to meet the stabling or grazing charges plus any feed costs, the farriery charges and the expense of regular worming.

It is advisable for you and the owner to have a written agreement detailing who insures the horse, who settles any veterinary bills, how much notice is required by either party before termination of the contract, who pays for saddlery repairs, how long the loan is for, and any particular restrictions relating to the use of the horse, such as whether the owner agrees to the animal being taken hunting. For the protection of all parties it is wise to pay a solicitor for his advice on drawing up a loan contract.

Loaning a horse can be a very enjoyable experience, provided you think and prepare ahead — and that includes preparing yourself for the inevitable parting once the owner has time to care for her horse again.

Buying your own horse

For many people it is the realization of a childhood dream when they finally ride out on their own horse. The pleasures of owning your own animal are countless, but it is also a huge responsibility and a big drain on financial resources. There is no way you can keep a horse cheaply. Of course you can save time and money if you are sensible, but if you think you can have a horse on a shoestring budget, forget it and start saving instead!

Before you start looking for a horse there are lots of points you need to consider. To begin with, could you really take on responsibility for an animal's life? Make no mistake about it, if you buy a horse the animal will be totally reliant upon you for food, water, shelter, exercise and everything connected with his mental and physical health. If the animal is ill at any time he will rely on you to notice the early warning signs that all is not well, and, having recognized a problem, to ensure that he receives the necessary expert attention.

It follows that in addition to being able to ride a horse you must also know how to look after one. If you are aiming to become a horse owner it is vital that you spend as much time as you can at your local school, helping with the animals, learning how to muck out, groom, get a horse fit, mix feeds, treat minor ailments and so on.

To give you an idea of what keeping your own horse involves would take another book. The point is that unless you have worked regularly with horses, have a good practical knowledge of stable management and horse health and have an open, enquiring mind, ever ready to learn more, then you would be better continuing as a weekly rider and forgetting horse ownership for a while.

Regular work with horses, either at your local riding school, or helping a private horse owner, will also educate you about the commitment of having a horse. He cannot be ignored when you go on holiday or fetch his own water and feed just because his owner is too lazy to leave the house on winter evenings.

If, after all that, you are undeterred and feel competent enough to cope with a horse, then before you rush off and buy one work out a budget. How much can you afford to spend on buying a horse? Have you added in the cost of having a prospective purchase vetted? Insurance is another necessity so do not forget to include a sum in your budget for this so that as soon as the horse is yours he is covered.

Do not forget that you have to get the horse from his current home to his new one. A saddle and bridle plus grooming kit, stable tools, feed and water buckets, head-collar and rope will also be needed. Has the horse been wormed regularly or vaccinated? Is he freeze-marked and, if not, are you going to take this precaution against theft?

Your horse will need feed, hay and bedding supplies too, plus somewhere to keep the feed dry and safe from vermin. The pounds soon add up, so try to think of every possible eventuality, including the horrible thought that the animal could quite possibly require veterinary attention.

It may seem rather obvious, but find somewhere to keep your horse before you buy him! Some people just rush in and then find that the only place they can conveniently reach provides only full livery which they cannot possibly afford. (A full livery service provides complete care, but it is very expensive.)

First-time owners will benefit considerably from joining a yard where the owner of the premises or other livery owners are experienced and friendly. Then you can pick their brains and turn to them for help if you are unsure about anything.

Work out the cost of travelling to and from your horse's home every day too. Petrol is a cost often overlooked, yet twice-daily trips can add up to a horrific fuel bill.

You may feel happier about entrusting your horse's care to someone else and putting the horse in full livery. This is the most expensive method and you need to ensure that you and the horse are receiving good service, but for some working horse owners it is the only way they can keep a horse. Both riding schools and private yards offer this kind of service.

Some schools operate a working livery system whereby the full livery fee is reduced because the school has use of your horse. While this means the horse is exercised if you are not available, it can create difficulties unless you and the school proprietor agree the number of hours which the horse is worked per day or week, when this work is carried out (you would not want your horse to be used in the school most of the weekend, for instance) and who will ride the horse.

Then it is wise to check regularly that everyone carries out their part of the deal. A big drawback with this system is that your horse is ridden by lots of different people — and possibly not all of them will be of a sufficiently high standard.

Do it yourself livery is just that — you hire a stable and/or use of grazing and you carry out all the other tasks yourself. In a yard where other owners have similar methods of horse management to you, it is a good idea to agree a rota system so you can all help each other therefore saving time and travelling expenses. For instance, one of you may feed, water, check over and turn out the horses in the morning while someone else does the evening duties. By sensible co-operation you can ensure that your horse is looked after properly and you still have time for all the other necessary tasks — like sleeping and eating!

If you have an animal which can live out all year round, it is obviously time-saving in that stable duties are not necessary. However, you do still need to visit at least twice daily. Any field also needs to have shelter, either a natural one, such as a good thick hedge, or a purpose-built one, to ensure that the horse has some protection from the elements, whether they be sun, driving rain or wind.

A water supply is vital, fencing needs to be secure, the grazing needs to be free of poisonous plants and there has to be sufficiently good grazing to support the number of animals. Horses like company, preferably their own kind or other grazing animals.

Having sorted out a home it is time to find the horse and that is no mean task! Anyone, and especially a first time buyer, needs to take along more experienced horse people to view prospective purchases.

It can be very easy to buy a totally unsuitable horse, so be prepared to look around and do not buy the first you see just because you are keen to have a horse.

Read all you can about conformation, health and anything you can find about buying horses; seek advice and keep your head when looking at animals. Take the time to find a suitable partner and then you and your horse can enjoy a great future together.

RIGHTS
AND WRONGS

Below *If you lead a horse or pony like this you can expect to get into trouble: the leader has very little control over the animal and is unable to either encourage him forwards or to check his speed if necessary. If anything were to startle the horse, the leader could well be knocked over.*

Bottom *Remember to run up stirrups when leading a tacked-up pony and position yourself alongside his shoulder for leading.*

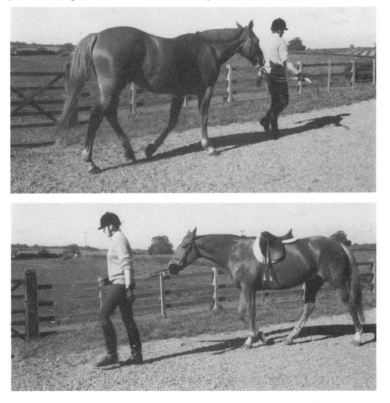

Left *Keep a good contact on your reins when mounting in order to prevent the horse moving off before you are 'on board'! Look back at the sequence showing how to mount correctly and you will avoid having to do contortions to get into the saddle.*

Right *Trying to haul yourself up using the saddle like this results in a damaged saddle which, if used, then makes the horse's back sore. As the rider has no rein contact the animal, who does not look at all happy with this unorthodox method of mounting, has moved off.*

Left *Training shoes are dangerous for riding, because if your foot slips through the stirrup iron you can be dragged and hurt. You must have proper riding boots or strong boots with a small heel.*

Above *Imagine riding all day, sitting like this! By simply sitting in the deepest part of the saddle and bringing her lower leg back, this rider will look better and be more effective. As she is sitting so far back on the saddle she will not be able to use her weight aids or back properly — and in addition she is making it more difficult for the horse to carry her easily.*

Below *Can you see how our rider has now brought up her heel and swung her lower leg too far back? This makes it difficult for her to give adequate instructions to the horse.*

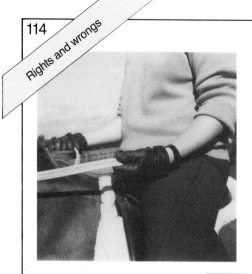

Left *What is wrong with the way these reins are held? Look back to page 47 for help if necessary.*

Right *It is quite common for riders to raise one hand higher than the other when riding circles, turns and so on. Be aware of where your hands are as you perform various exercises. A quick test is to place a whip across your hands, held in place by your thumbs: if you do raise one hand more than the other it will soon become evident.*

Left *Washing line reins are a problem with beginner riders: some people find it difficult to keep the reins at a suitable length and seem to let the reins slip through their fingers. Refer back to the section on holding the reins — if you ride with reins like this you will not be able to control your horse properly.*

Above *Do not let a riding school put you on a pony that is too small for you — it is not fair to you or the pony! This rider would not be able to use her legs properly to give any aids as her lower leg is well below the pony's sides.*

Below *Spot two obvious mistakes in this example of how not to tighten a girth!*

Left A potential accident here: imagine the horse throwing up his head just as the rider was bringing her leg over his neck! She would be knocked off backwards, but her left foot is still in the stirrup iron so she could easily be dragged along. With such long reins it is also possible that she could get her right foot caught in them, injuring her and frightening the horse.

Right This way of dismounting is safer but still not correct. Look at the horse's obvious displeasure as his rider clambers off instead of springing lightly from the saddle.

Left Riding with stirrups which are too long means that you have to reach for your irons and so you are less stable in the saddle and less effective.

Right *The position of your foot in the stirrup is an important part of your overall riding position. Here the rider barely has her toe in the iron so it would be very easy for her whole foot to keep slipping out of the iron, so unbalancing her.*

Left *Ramming your foot home in the iron is also not advisable. Look at how the incorrect placing has affected the rest of the girl's leg position.*

Right *Here the rider has turned out her lower legs and toes, to give the horse an aid instead of simply closing her legs around the horse's sides.*

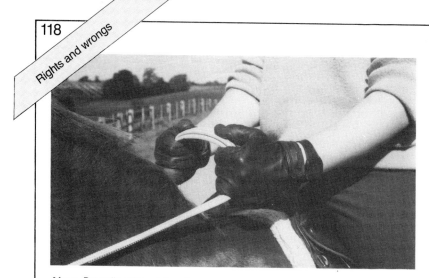

Above Rounding the wrists sets up resistance in the hands, making them tense and less able to follow the movements of the horse's head sympathetically.

Right What has happened to the straight line from the horse's mouth through the reins to the rider's hands? See how this ideal has been ruined by holding the reins too high.

Left The rider's hands are still too high, but the reins do not look quite so bad because the rider is rising too high to the trot! Beginners often try to haul themselves up in rising trot using the reins when they should be letting the movement of the horse's body help them. Try not to work too hard at rising — you do not need to be this far out of the saddle.

Right Another common problem — as the rider has approached the corner she has collapsed her upper body, brought up her lower leg, and turned out her toe. She has slumped in the saddle and will have to work harder from this position to give any aids than if she was sitting correctly.

Left Here the rider is leaning too far back and her hands are set. She will not be the easiest of burdens for the horse to carry, and will find it extremely difficult to rise to the trot properly as she will always be 'behind the movement' of the horse.

Right Leaning too far forward and collapsing your back also brings its problems. The rider here is not very secure and could easily be unseated, if, for example, the horse tripped or shied. Her incorrect position also makes it difficult for her to give effective aids, so it is well worth taking the time to acquire a reasonable riding position. Look at the rider's arms — they are flapping around instead of lightly touching her sides.

Above Failure to obtain canter results from a lack of preparation by the rider. For instance here the horse is not working actively enough (his hind feet ought to be coming down in the tracks made by his forefeet) and he is not really concentrating. Look at the positional faults of the rider.

Below Riders can become over-anxious when they ask for canter, leaning forwards in an attempt to encourage their horse. This does not work as the rider is unable to use her aids properly and usually the horse just trots faster and faster.

Above Another common fault is to look down to check whether your horse is cantering on the correct leg. With practice you will be able to feel whether the horse is correct or not, but if you do need to check, a glance down should be sufficient. Leaning down like this unbalances the horse and also makes it very obvious to anyone watching that the rider is not over-confident.

Below Spot the deliberate mistake here! Check back to page 48 if you need any help.

Above Keep your distance! Riding like this, whether in a school, along a road or bridleway, is asking for trouble.

Right How to make life difficult for the horse when riding uphill! Try to help not hinder, and take your weight off the horse's back.

Left It is just as important to assist your horse going downhill. Do not hang on to his mouth, but keep an even contact and let your body go with the movement of the horse.

Right If you try and go over a fence like this your chances of staying on are pretty slim! The rider's stirrups are too short so his bottom is well out of the saddle with his knees well above the knee flaps. If he needed to grip in an emergency there would be nothing to grip!

Left A common problem when jumping is for the rider to throw his lower legs back so weakening his security.

Right You can see here that the rider has no secure base — his legs are too far back, he is too far out of the saddle and his upper body is well forward. The jumping position has been exaggerated here and the rider will again find it difficult to stay in balance with the horse.

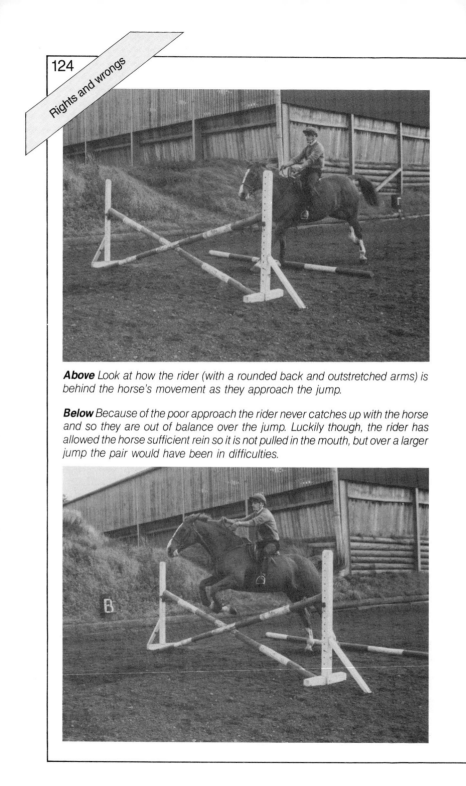

Above *Look at how the rider (with a rounded back and outstretched arms) is behind the horse's movement as they approach the jump.*

Below *Because of the poor approach the rider never catches up with the horse and so they are out of balance over the jump. Luckily though, the rider has allowed the horse sufficient rein so it is not pulled in the mouth, but over a larger jump the pair would have been in difficulties.*

Above Here the opposite is happening, with the rider throwing himself forward in an exaggerated position and leaning to one side.

Below As they land you can see the effect of the rider slipping out to one side — both horse and rider are unbalanced and would find it hard to gather themselves up sufficiently and be prepared for another fence if, for instance, they were jumping a double or treble.

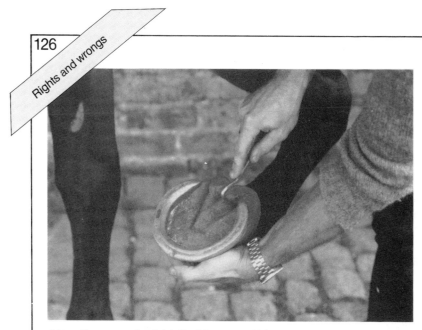

Above *If you use a hoofpick like this you could damage the frog — the sensitive v-shaped part of the horse's foot.*

Below *As soon as a rider sits in this saddle it will press down on the horse's back making him sore and uncomfortable. All tack should be regularly checked for correct fit, as a damaged back could put a horse out of action for a long time.*

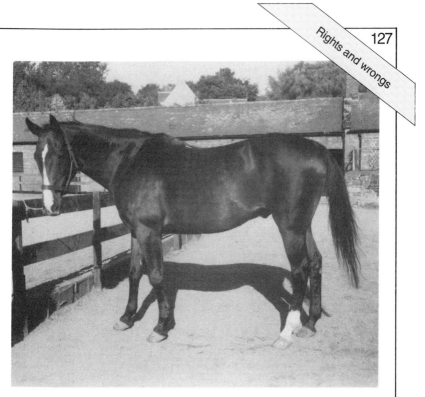

Above Never tie a horse to a solid object, but attach breakable string first and tie the horse up to the string loop. That way the horse can break free if necessary. Think of the consequences if something terrified this horse and he could not break free.

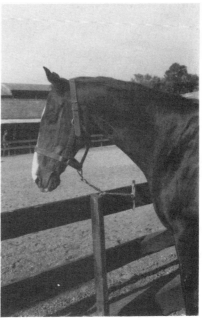

Right Always use quick release knots so that if there is an emergency you can release the horse speedily. By using this type of knot you could have a terrified and injured horse.

USEFUL ADDRESSES

Arab Horse Society
Goddards Green, Cranbrook,
Kent TN17 3LP

Association of British Riding Schools
Old Brewery Yard, Penzance,
Cornwall, TR18 2SL

British Horse Society
British Equestrian Centre,
Stoneleigh, Warwickshire,
CV8 2LR

Coloured Horse & Pony Breed Society
15 Wilga Road, Welwyn, Herts

Dales Pony Society
55 Cromwell Street, Walkley,
Sheffield, S6 3RN

Dartmoor Pony Society
Weston Manor, Corscombe,
Dorchester, Dorset, DT2 0PB

English Connemara Pony Society
2 The Leys, Salford, Chipping
Norton, Oxon

Exmoor Pony Society
Quarry Cottage, Sampford
Brett, Williton, Somerset

Fell Pony Society
19 Dragley Beck, Ulverston,
Cumbria, LA12 0HD

Irish Draught Horse Society
Fourth Street, National
Agricultural Centre, Stoneleigh,
Warks, CV8 2LG

New Forest Pony & Cattle Breeding Society
Beacon Corner, Burley,
Ringwood, Hants, BH24 4EW

Pony Club
British Equestrian Centre,
Stoneleigh, Warks, CV8 2LR

Premier Farmkey
Universal House, Riverside,
Banbury, Oxon, OX16 8TF

Riding for the Disabled Association
Avenue R, National Agricultural
Centre, Kenilworth, Warks, CV8
2LY

Shetland Pony Stud Book Society
8 Whinfield Road, Montrose,
Angus, DD10 8SA

Thoroughbred Breeders Assn
Stanstead House, The Avenue,
Newmarket, Suffolk, CB8 9AA

Welsh Pony & Cob Society
6 Chalybeate Street,
Aberystwyth, Dyfed, SY23 1HS